When Life Tumbles In

Also by C. Welton Gaddy
published by Westminster/John Knox Press

*A Soul Under Siege:
Surviving Clergy Depression*

When Life Tumbles In

Westminster/John Knox Press
Louisville, Kentucky

© 1993 C. Welton Gaddy

All rights reserved. No part of this book may be reproduced or transmitted in any form or by any means, electronic or mechanical, including photocopying, recording, or by any information storage or retrieval system, without permission in writing from the publisher. For information, address Westminster/John Knox Press, 100 Witherspoon Street, Louisville, Kentucky 40202-1396.

Scripture quotations from the New Revised Standard Version of the Bible are copyright © 1989 by the Division of Christian Education of the National Council of the Churches of Christ in the U.S.A., and are used by permission.

Book design by Drew Stevens

First edition

Published by Westminster/John Knox Press
Louisville, Kentucky

This book is printed on acid-free paper that meets the American National Standards Institute Z39.48 standard. ∞

PRINTED IN THE UNITED STATES OF AMERICA
9 8 7 6 5 4 3 2 1

Library of Congress Cataloging-in-Publication Data

Gaddy, C. Welton.
    When life tumbles in : a handbook for coping / C. Welton Gaddy.
— 1st ed.
      p.   cm.
  Includes bibliographical references.
  ISBN 0–664–25458–6 (alk. paper)

  1. Suffering—Religious aspects—Christianity. 2. Life change events—Religious aspects—Christianity. 3. Adjustment (Psychology)—Religious aspects—Christianity. 4. Christian life—1960– I. Title.
BV4908.5.G33   1993
248.8'6—dc20   93–8021

CONTENTS

INTRODUCTION		1
ONE	Be Honest About Your Situation	7
TWO	Get Plenty of Rest	23
THREE	Reach Out to Friends	36
FOUR	Fight Cynicism	49
FIVE	Keep a Sense of Humor	57
SIX	Pray	65
SEVEN	Channel Your Anger	74
EIGHT	Renew Your Dreams	82
NINE	Exercise Faith	90
TEN	Offer Help to Someone Else	101
EPILOGUE		110
NOTES		112

When Life Tumbles In

INTRODUCTION

An old proverb—Scottish, I think—declares, "Never morning wore to evening lest some heart did break." Amen! most people exclaim. Or, You can say that again!

Perhaps the accuracy of the proverb can be debated theoretically. But not practically. Everyone knows its validity. All people hurt at one time or another. No exceptions.

Sources of hurt vary as much as do the people who experience pain. Some difficulties make front-page news: A loss of security for employees of a company that has filed for bankruptcy. Personal reputations jeopardized by a corporation's ruthless hostile-takeover strategy. Radically reduced income for many families because of massive personnel layoffs at the local factory. Bitter defeat in a viciously contested local election. Dismissal from the leadership board of a charitable agency that has been losing money. The shame of volatile conflict within a church. Embarrassment over a bad decision involving public funds. Outright charges of incompetency by colleagues.

Other problems remain more private, though no less painful: the breakup of a marriage, forced termination from a job, identity confusion, betrayal by a friend, an eruption of doubt, a loss of self-confidence, exposure of an illicit love affair, the death of a family member, despondency bordering on depression, dependency on drugs, rumors that threaten to ruin a good reputation, a spouse who is no longer liked, much less loved, rejection by a son or a daughter, a debilitating illness, a vocational crisis.

Such difficulties create a level of hurt that precipitates

predictable reactions. Stress intensifies. Frayed emotions find expression in denial, depression, guilt, withdrawal, self-hatred, frustration, or paranoia. Frequently persons traumatized by life-altering situations experience disorientation and confusion. Anger erupts apart from any apparent reason. Trust, both in systems and persons, breaks down completely. Life seems out of control. It may be.

Crises assault a person totally—emotionally, spiritually, and physically. They brutally batter an individual's ego, so that little or no sense of self-worth survives. A crisis tests both short-term agendas and long-range dreams. Ultimate and penultimate concerns merge so completely that little distinction can be made between questions about what to do today and what to do about life. Feelings about one's job get all mixed up with feelings about one's self. Convictions are questioned or abandoned. Courage recedes. Values fluctuate wildly.

Crisis-plagued persons lose confidence in other people and are devastated by a reciprocal diminution of confidence on the part of others. Large public gatherings intimidate those who are in pain. They prize solitude as much as they despise it. Problem-wearied persons often want to give up. Some do.

Since a major crisis affects an individual holistically, only a holistic response to a crisis really helps. To be effective, coping must be comprehensive.

Sharing Pain

In the following chapters you will find ten suggestions for coping with a crisis. None is based on theory alone. All are rooted in experience—my personal experience and the experiences of those who have invited me to share in their struggles with a wide variety of problems.

Many scholarly volumes address in great detail most of the issues briefly discussed here. Research in that literature has been a part of my work, but only a minor part. The insights and recommendations that follow come more from an engagement with personal pain than from academic investigation. My own reflections on personal experiences form the basis of this book.

Each crisis-oriented suggestion in this volume has proven beneficial to me. I know firsthand the terrain of trouble. I have been frightened by the terror of a threatening situation, frozen by the shock of unexpected pain, immobilized by difficulties that held no promise of a good solution, racked by anxieties about the future, angered by persons (often well-meaning) who told me everything was going to be all right, and devastated by the notion that no one else really understood my plight or could be counted on to stand by me in dealing with it. I have been besieged by panic as I sought to regain a measure of equilibrium when the bottom of my life fell away and sent me plummeting in free fall toward God knows what. I scrambled to cover the nakedness I felt when life was suddenly stripped of all its normal sources of security, I tried to force a confession of solid religious conviction when my spiritual faith mirrored the turmoil of my physical or emotional condition, and, yes, I tried to take care of myself with no help from anyone else.

In an earlier book titled *A Soul Under Siege,* I sketched the dimensions of my difficulties. When distress and hurt are confessed, each becomes a pole around which communion develops. Shared pain forms a strong foundation for community. Since the publication of my autobiographical statement about crisis, innumerable persons have trusted me to listen to their cries of pain. Our conversations have produced a fellowship oriented toward the improvement, if not the complete cure (or resolution), of their troubled situations.

I invite you to join those conversations. By means of this book, I would like to establish a form of camaraderie with you. As I write, I am envisioning the faces of specific people—those who have sat across the room from me pouring out their problems one-on-one and those who gathered in front of a lectern in a conference room ready to listen for a word of help and then share their troubles. Similarly, I am recalling the sounds of faceless voices addressing me from the other end of a telephone line. I have in mind people like you. I write with an intense desire to offer guidance that can help you deal positively with the crisis (or crises) fracturing your world and sending its shattered fragments tumbling down around you.

Caution

Please note two words of caution.

First, if your crisis involves mental or physical illness, chemical problems, addictive or abusive behavior, illegal activities, or long-term relational difficulties, this book cannot be a substitute for seeking therapy from a competent professional trained to treat your special need. Your road to crisis resolution may lead through a hospital or some other institution for healing. Extensive therapy may be an essential ingredient in sustaining the stability and fulfillment you seek in life. Facilities, programs, and personnel for problem-solving are gifts from God. Take advantage of them with gratitude for their availability.

My own path to better health wound its way through a hospital. Therapeutic checkups continue. Had I not traveled that road, I doubt this book would have been written. Ironically, we often discover basic resources for health, wholeness, and happiness—resources for coping—amid a journey through horrendous hurt. Certainly better and easier ways to find them exist. But apparently some of us have to see life at its worst before realizing what about life is best.

No substitutes exist for assistance from professional caregivers. However, attentiveness to the suggestions that follow can complement the work of professionals. It did for me.

A second word of caution: This is not a self-help book.

Self-help during a crisis is important, indeed a necessity. However, persons caught up in crises need more assistance than can be found in individual resources. In the final analysis, coping with difficulties is an extremely personal matter. But

INTRODUCTION

help from other people and an openness to God (or the lack thereof) contribute significantly to a person's coping skills.

Frankly, I have no concept of a self-made person. The adjective "self-made" contradicts the true nature of the noun "person." To be sure, heroic achievements by strong-willed individuals receive public acclaim from time to time. But to confuse such personal successes with individual self-sufficiency is a serious mistake. Everybody needs other people. No individual becomes a healthy person alone.

"Bootstrap salvation" defies understanding, at least for me. Even the image presents problems. How does one reach down and pull oneself up by one's own bootstraps? So garbled a statement indicates the nature of the thought behind it. Individuals must exert initiative in working through a crisis, but salvation does not take place apart from the assistance of others (divine or human).

Periodically, a popular saying makes the rounds, either as a personal confession or as a general recommendation. Someone declares, "If life hands you a lemon, make lemonade." Most listeners immediately think, Wow! What a great attitude. What terrific advice! Really?

No doubt this clever suggestion represents the best advice of adherents to the power-of-positive-thinking philosophy and advocates of aggressive self-assertion. It sounds good. But how does it fare amid a storm? When a mother hears that her son has killed himself, can she be comforted and helped to cope with this horrible fact by an admonition to make lemonade? What about a man who loses all his retirement funds and other life savings?

You need water to make lemonade. Without it, you have only lemon juice. Can you create water? And what about the sourness of water mixed with this lemon juice? Good lemonade requires a sweetener. Can self-will produce an antidote to bitterness? Be realistic about making lemonade—and about coping with crises.

Self-help can take a person only so far, then assistance is

needed. A do-it-yourself approach to life seriously misinterprets the nature of both personhood and life.

I encourage—indeed insist on—self-help. Each of my ten suggestions for coping involves individual initiative. But in no way do I want to suggest that you can successfully negotiate your way through a crisis on the basis of self-sufficiency alone.

Two basic assumptions undergrid the recommendations in this volume: Every person needs other people, and all people need God.

Direct counsel follows. I have made no effort to be subtle. However, the explicit manner in which I write should not suggest a personal smugness about rightness that disdains alternative views. My hope is to be provocative and prodding in service to the larger goal of offering help. At no point do I expect my advice to be accepted uncritically. What has worked for me may not work for you. Please criticize my assumptions, question my conclusions, disagree with my directions, and evaluate every word of my counsel. Accept what you can. Dismiss what you must. But please do not take these recommendations lightly or ignore them.

My arrangement of the chapters suggests no order of priority. All ten statements of advice are important in the coping process. You may find one of them to be more significant than the others at a particular point in a crisis. However, each of the suggestions elaborated here has helped me immensely. I am convinced they can help you.

CHAPTER ONE

Be Honest About Your Situation

Crises prompt panic. Watch out. Panic produces extreme reactions that are devoid of the honest appraisal of your situation that is so necessary.

Though threatened to the core of your being or troubled to the point of despair, you may deny that anything is wrong. People in critical situations often remark, "Oh, I'm fine. Everything is all right. Don't worry about me."

Denial is only one of several defense mechanisms commonly used by individuals seeking to avoid an honest confrontation with their problems. Other options for evasion include:

Rationalization: You convince yourself and others that the situation is not really what it seems to be
Repression: You push all troubles from your mind
Displacement: You shift your reactions from one subject to another
Projection: You attribute your thoughts, motives, and actions to other people
Reaction formation: You substitute an acceptable feeling or motive for its opposite.[1]

Hyperbolic thinking about a crisis also hurts the cause of honesty and is an immediate danger sign. Some people may oversimplify the nature of a problem: "This is just a little misunderstanding that will be corrected as soon as I talk to the appropriate people." Others may overstate the problem's severity: "My life is ruined forever!"

Guard against cock-eyed optimism, blind escapism, or

Chicken Little negativism. None of the three supports an appropriate response to a major crisis. Face squarely the untouched-up truths related to your problem. Coping with a situation effectively—any situation—requires looking at it honestly. No hedging.

Before his untimely death, my good friend Grady Nutt regularly made me laugh and learn at the same time. One of his stories makes a powerful comment about this matter of honesty during a crisis.

A huge fire was burning out of control in a warehouse of monstrous dimensions. Observers watched listlessly, almost immobilized by fear. Fire fighters on the scene were making little or no progress in extinguishing the flames. Panic made the owner of the building frantic. In desperation he offered a reward of ten thousand dollars to anyone who could save his property.

Immediately, one of the bystanders suggested that a call for assistance be made to the smallest fire company in town. All around people responded with derisive laughter. But in this rapidly worsening situation, no source of help could be spurned. Someone placed the call.

Almost momentarily, it seemed, a small red fire truck squealed around the corner with sirens screaming full blast and fire fighters hanging on for dear life. When the little truck approached the blazing warehouse, it did not stop. Everyone gasped. The fire engine crashed right through the outer wall of the building.

Amazed onlookers could see fire fighters inside the inferno rapidly working to quench the flames. Word spread quickly through loud shouts: "They are fighting the fire from the inside out!" No one had seen anything like this ever before.

Later, after the fire had been contained and extinguished, the fire chief who saved the day stood talking with reporters. He was commended for his courage. The grateful owner of the warehouse wanted to go on record stating that this was the bravest fire company in the world. Everybody marveled at the fact that the fire was fought from the inside out.

Ceremoniously, the warehouse owner presented a check for ten thousand dollars to the battered-looking fire chief. He was a pitiable sight. Ashes and smoke covered him from head to toe. His helmet, coat, and boots had been melted by the intense heat. Handing over the reward, the warehouse owner asked, "I would like for you to tell us what you plan to do with this money." The beleaguered fire chief responded humbly, but with obvious satisfaction, "I don't know what we'll do with all of it, but the first thing we're going to do is buy some new brakes for that truck!"

All efforts to cope with a major problem require honesty. Don't talk about courage if bad brakes are the issue. Focusing on unrealistic matters worsens a situation rather than helps it. Truth is a non-negotiable, an essential ingredient, in responsible coping.[2]

Ask Hard Questions

Asking the right questions about a crisis takes you at least halfway down the road to discovering the truths that must be known in order to cope with a crisis effectively. This task may appear simple and easy to accomplish. Don't believe it. Establishing factual information inevitably involves raising hard questions about the problem—mind-boggling, gut-wrenching, tough questions. Troubled by difficulties we already recognize, we have to search for data we would just as soon not know. But search we must. What we don't know can hurt us much more than what we do know.

Crises differ dramatically. For this reason, the nature of each situation dictates the specific questions that need to be asked regarding it.

A man badly shaken by his doctor's diagnosis of a serious illness can benefit immensely from focusing on factual data (as opposed to spending time pondering what is rumored, feared, or imagined). Questions point the way: What did the doctor actually say about my condition? Did other people in the room at the time hear exactly what I heard? What do I face? Can I expect to feel better or worse in the days immediately ahead? How must I alter my lifestyle, if at all? What finances will I need to cover the costs of my treatment?

A woman fired from a professional position may be tempted to lash out at her former employer. "I'm the victim of an unfair system, an expendable pawn. I got caught between two corporate executives battling each other for power." She might assume that she won't have any trouble finding new work. "Anybody can understand what happened to me." She is placing her confidence in a dangerous assumption, which needs to be evaluated by asking and answering hard questions. "Was there any good reason (even arguably good) for my termination? Are my resentment, judgment, and confidence informed by facts?" She must know the answers to these questions.

Other essential inquiries for this troubled woman include: "Can I get a good letter of recommendation from my former employer? Will my former colleagues say anything that will hurt my chances for reemployment and, if so, what? Do the financial arrangements in my termination agreement reflect appreciation and goodwill or a hostile 'good riddance'?" Without accurate answers to these questions, this woman can be blindsided by more hurt as she begins her search for a new job.

Whether functioning alone in the privacy of your home or in a place under public scrutiny, surrounded by strangers or family members, whether struggling with a lack of institutional support or with the loss of a personal relationship, certain kinds of questions apply to almost every difficult situation.

Definition questions. Precisely what is the problem? (No generalities.) How bad is it? What is the most threatening aspect of this situation? How real is that threat? How imminent? In what ways will the materialization of this threat affect my family, my work, and my reputation?

Relational questions. Who supports me? Who opposes me? Whom can I count on to help me? What kind of support from these people can I realistically expect?

Political questions. Who believes me? Does my point of view represent that of a majority or a minority of the people involved? Among those who believe me, who will actually go to bat for me? Who are my enemies? What negative forces must I confront and overcome in order to resolve this matter successfully? Are there any political alliances or compromises I should consider?

Resources questions. What are my resources (emotional, social, financial, spiritual, and mental) for responding to this situation? How likely is a change for the better, if not a resolution of the matter? Might this occur quickly? If not, how long can I last? Is winning this battle worth what the victory will cost? What are my immediate needs? Where can I turn for help?

Coping with a crisis is difficult even when you know virtually everything about it. A lack of realism about your problem, however, severely reduces any prospects for finding a healthy solution to it. You have virtually no chance of successfully coping with a bad situation if you are unsure or unaware of the precise dimensions of the difficulty, the size of the most formidable obstacles to be overcome, and the inherent political dynamics that can either aid you or hinder you.

For goodness' sake (literally), ask questions about your difficulties. Ask the kind of tough questions whose answers will yield information to aid the coping process and save you from unnecessary hurt.

Examine Generalizations

Better counsel urges, "Avoid generalizations entirely." But that advice is useless. You will make generalizations from time to time. Everybody does. Typically, the worse you feel, the more sweeping and inaccurate your statements will be. So examine all your generalizations (as well as those of others). Keep in mind that honesty is the goal.

Crises evoke predictable statements from those involved.

Each merits careful study: "I have never felt worse than I do today," "My situation is hopeless," "I don't believe anyone else has ever experienced such hurt and betrayal of their love," "My life is over," "I know I will never get beyond the grief caused by this loss."

Listen carefully to your comments. Then ask if you really mean what you have said. If your words accurately reflect the truth as you see it, stay with your statement. The dramatic nature of your remark reveals the severity of your condition and the depth of your need for help. However, if, after taking a closer look, you see what you have said is an overstatement of your situation, admit it. Admit it to yourself and to any other people who heard your first declaration.

Crises involve dynamics that are bad enough without exaggeration. Be as cautious about overstating the negatives of your situation as you are about glamorizing the positives related to it. Do not sell yourself a bill of goods at either extreme. What you gain immediately by such a purchase cannot compare with the inordinate price you will eventually have to pay.

Stark honesty about your situation exists as one of your greatest allies and most valuable resources in the coping process. Generalizations do not help at all.

Distinguish Between What Should Be and What Is

Hypotheses help little when facing a crisis. Naïvieté can be destructive. Coping successfully with a problem requires confronting what is, rather than dwelling on what could be or what should be.

Some people make religious convictions an exception to this rule. They are not. Christian hope differs significantly from wishful thinking. Practicing a childlike faith does not mean behaving childishly. An ignorance of facts fails to qualify as admirable piety.

BE HONEST ABOUT YOUR SITUATION

A series of newspaper articles embarrasses a civic official by charging him with professional misconduct. Initially, the man finds comfort in thinking, Across the years, I have helped so many people in trouble, some of them will surely step forward now in my defense. That makes sense. But it is probably not true. Eventually this public figure must ask, "Where are those people I have helped? Who actually gives me support?" If no one steps forward to offer assistance, the official must scrap his initial surmise and begin to help himself. Whether or not that is the way the situation should be, that is the way the situation *is*.

A young man grieves over the loss of a woman he considers the love of his life. Grasping to find some way out of his devastation, the fellow says to himself, "I am a pretty strong person. I ought to be able to put my life back together by myself and get on with something else." Maybe so. But is it true? Does the betrayed lover have the resources necessary to assure sufficient self-help? If not, he must deal with the reality of his life rather than with what he thinks should be.

Caught up in a crisis, you may convince yourself: "My friends ought to provide enough grace (substitute *comfort, reassurance, support,* or whatever you need) for me to get through this bad time, "My church should be a conduit of divine mercy and forgiveness committed to my restoration," or "My employer ought to understand emotional trauma enough not to terminate my position during this period of economic difficulty." Beware. You are right to bring to mind such "oughts" and "shoulds." But healthy coping with your difficulties demands that you discover if what *should* be is synonymous with reality. If not, acknowledge the truth. Let your sad conclusion—that help is not where it ought to be—serve as a prelude to searching vigorously for help elsewhere.

Effective coping does not trade in wishful thinking (even if it sounds like noble religious belief). Neither does it depend on thoughts that are right theoretically (theologically, biblically, ecclesiastically) but without counterparts in actual fact.

Coping demands an honest recognition of reality.

Weigh Carefully Other People's Advice

You need counsel from other people, especially in a time of crisis. Insights from those around you can be very beneficial. Helpful counsel from other people is not a sure thing, though. Sometimes the advice of others hurts more than it helps. You must weigh carefully the opinions of nonprofessionals, particularly those recommendations that come from individuals who barely know you (mine included).

People who stand outside your crisis do not always have an objective view of the situation. Distance from a problem does not automatically guarantee an accurate definition of the problem. Individuals can parade prejudices, reactionary attitudes, and simmering anger before you as dispassionate, unbiased counsel. Watch out. A failure to identify these phenomena correctly will hamper successful coping.

Occasionally another's advice represents more a projection of that person's problems, sentiments, and aspirations than observations tailored to help you cope with your own troubles. Consider an incident based on actual experience. After an extended period of fatigue and melancholy, you take a leave of absence from work in order to rest and recover. A coworker advises you, "Once you get out of this place, don't come back. Use your time off to look for another job. Leave this rat race behind you." The colleague seems to mean well. However, in reality, the advice is based on what the coworker wants to do rather than on what you yourself may or may not need to do.

You know yourself. You can get in touch with your priorities, aspirations, and goals even if they are unclear at a given moment. Weigh the counsel received from others over against what you know about yourself. Be honest enough about yourself to evaluate advice from other people: "That thought is worth pursuing; her suggestion can really help me"; "I need to think more about his counsel before I act on it"; "That advice is not for me. Though offered with good intentions, my friend's

BE HONEST ABOUT YOUR SITUATION

counsel involves a course of action that will do me more harm than good."

Be careful. You do not really cope with a crisis or solve a problem when your response hinges on attempts to live as someone other than who you are. If following other people's advice takes you where you do not feel you belong, involves you in actions that violate your conscience, or places you in a position that compromises your sense of personal integrity, beware. Better still, stop. Compliance with such counsel will enlarge your problem and create major new difficulties rather than facilitate helpful coping.

Not uncommonly, some of the worst advice offered amid a crisis comes from well-meaning people and sounds good. Wearied by your struggles, you may be attracted to the counsel of a longtime friend who says, "Don't worry about this situation. God will work it out. Everything is going to be all right." How many times I have heard such comments and desperately wanted to believe them! But look closely at that advice. Take it apart piece by piece and study it.

Being told not to worry is useless, as well as insensitive. Faced by a bad situation that could get worse rapidly, you will worry. You *should* worry. With the outcome of a crisis still in question and your security seriously threatened, anxiety is a sign of health rather than sickness. Don't think twice about your worry or feel guilty because you have it.

Nobody can tell you that everything will be all right without your personally taking any initiative in problem-solving or coping. That advice is ridiculous; it is not an indication of good faith but a revelation of incredible stupidity. Positive thinking merits commendation. But realistic thinking helps more—whether such thoughts are positive or negative.

Common sense ranks among God's greatest gifts, and it is most valuable during a crisis. Use it. God will not work out everything for you (or for anyone else), functioning as a cosmic bellhop or a heaven-based Mr. Fixit. God will work with you and does work within you as you confront perplexing problems. In fact, God already has provided for your most basic needs in the face of trouble—instilling within you a capacity to exercise reason and assuring you of a divine, loving presence that will not forsake you, whether your thoughts are accurate or wrong. But you must think and act for yourself.

Glib counsel must be exposed. Effective coping skills trade in truth. Clarifying bad counsel qualifies as a profoundly religious act. It establishes truth, truth that you need and truth that, according to the Bible, sets you free: truth, not cheery thoughts or bad theology.

Advice from people around you will be plentiful. Some of it can help. Some of it can hurt. Consider all of it carefully.

Get in Touch with Your Feelings

Emotional honesty is as essential as intellectual honesty in coping with difficulties. But it may be more difficult to determine.

Mental tapes that play culturally conditioned counsel encourage emotional dishonesty: "Keep a stiff upper lip," "Don't let other people see your hurt," "Good people don't get angry," "Repress your emotions and exalt reason."

Comments commonly heard in public exert a strong negative influence on disturbed individuals: "Look how strong she is, not shedding a tear during the funeral"; "I admire that man so much. With his life crumbling before his eyes, he always wears a smile and acts as if things could not be better."

Recently I listened to two people talk about forced termination from their jobs. One had served as a parish pastor. Both individuals described despicable examples of unfairness, insensitivity, and injustice on the part of their former employers. Occasionally, anger flashed in their eyes and resentment shot through their speech.

BE HONEST ABOUT YOUR SITUATION

During a dialogue period, a member of the audience asked the former pastor to talk about his feelings related to the church that dismissed him. At first, the fellow continued to recite a litany of his pain. Then, suddenly, as if a cerebral tape clicked on, reminding him of proper expectations, the man changed his demeanor and words entirely. He began saying what he thought he ought to say. "But those are good people in that congregation. I'm not mad at them. I still love that church." Some people seated around me remarked about the man's marvelous attitude. I watched his knotty body language. As I listened to his words, I felt sad that the fellow could not own up in public to his anger and grief.

In his work *Dr. Zhivago,* Boris Pasternak wrote, "Your health is bound to be affected if, day after day, you say the opposite of what you feel, if you grovel before what you dislike and rejoice at what brings you nothing but misfortune. Our nervous system . . . can't be forever violated with impunity."[3] Exactly.

Often we try so hard to fool other people about our emotions that we become victims of our own lies. Asked how we are doing in the face of major difficulties, we feel our innards drowning in anxiety but we say, "Great. I'm doing just fine. I hope you are." A friend wants to know if she can do anything to help. An awareness of pressing needs surfaces immediately, only to be pushed aside by a macho mentality that dictates the declaration of a deadly fabrication: "No thanks. Everything is all right. Things are getting better every day." You can convey such lies to others so frequently and intensely that you begin to believe them yourself.

Self-deception comes easily, but it is destructive. A lack of emotional honesty not only hinders the coping process, it saps personal strength and erodes the capacity to deal successfully with what is wrong.

Express your grief. Declare your disappointment. Admit your anger. Confess your hurt. Talk about your fear. Face into your fatigue.

If you need to cry, do not hold back the tears. Speak about your confusion. Expose your desire for help. If you sense the need to laugh, laugh.

Other people may not understand either your feelings or the manner in which you express them. So what? Your emotions do not have to make sense, even to you. Most crises consist of innumerable irrational components. You are under no obligation to explain or justify your emotions. Your feelings are yours. Be honest about them. Express them.

Emotional honesty provides an accurate depiction of your internal condition—a condition that may demand further attention even as it enhances your capabilities for coping. The alternative worsens your present problems and creates additional difficulties.

Separate Your Trouble from Your Worth

Trouble in your life does not destroy your value as an individual. Sins and errors only confirm the fact that you are a finite, fallible human being. That truth should come as no surprise, only as a confirmation of what you have known about yourself ever since the time you could know yourself at all. You are an error maker. You are a sinner. Just like everybody else.

Symptoms of the human condition do not—cannot—rob you of your inherent value as a person. Individual worth is a gift from God, the God in whose image all people are created. And God does not offer come-and-go gifts willy-nilly. Human value cannot be taken away. You are a person of dignity and worth. That's that.

"Have my difficulties developed because of my wrongdoing?" you ask. Maybe. Maybe not. Immorality frequently results in personal crises. A decade of cheating on income tax returns precipitates a legal and financial crisis of major proportions. A series of broken promises stirs up a nearly unstillable storm of distrust. But that is not the whole story.

BE HONEST ABOUT YOUR SITUATION

Some problems defy easy explanations. Over and over, I have hurt badly while listening to sufferers' pain-laced questions: "Did God take the life of our infant daughter because of my immoral behavior?" "Am I having to face one crisis after another because God wants to get even with me?" No! Absolutely not. Those inquiries embrace, at least implicitly, a pagan view of life that distorts the nature of God as revealed in the Bible and prevents a proper understanding of personhood. No simplistic cosmic arrangement guarantees that within our lives good will always be rewarded with more good and evil punished with something bad. All too often, awfully bad things happen to extremely good people.

Good behavior carries no assurance of an absence of hurt. Rabbi Harold Kushner relates the observation of one of his teachers: "Expecting the world to treat you fairly because you are a good person is like expecting the bull not to charge you because you are a vegetarian."[4] Right.

Conversely, the presence of difficulties in your life is not a sure sign of wrongdoing. The author of the biblical book of Job tried to make this truth unforgettable centuries ago. We ought to know it by now. Historically, many of our greatest moral heroes have endured horrendous personal difficulties.

You can rightfully feel sorrow because of the crisis you face and regret over your contributions to it. However, you cannot legitimately feel despondent about who you are. That is not your call. Bad judgments, immoral actions, and questionable decisions do not negate your individual worth and the potential for its expression. God endows you with value as a person. And God did not err in establishing you as an individual of infinite worth.

Your present situation, whatever its nature, cannot rob you of God's gift of personal value. Neither can it destroy the accompanying God-given strength for coping that allows you to look to the future with vibrant hope.

Please do not confuse these remarks on personal value with

optimistic platitudes produced by the power of positive thinking, a tricky strategy intended to throw the best possible light on a bad situation. Personal worth is a matter of God's truth. So are the promise and power for coping inherent in your worth as a person.

Do You Want to Get Well?

"Do I want to get well? What a ridiculous question! Are you trying to be cruel?"

That may be your initial (and understandable) response to this piercing inquiry. However, a commitment to total honesty about your situation demands a straightforward answer, not a defensive reaction. That question takes dead aim at a clarification of the nature of your will.

Jesus first raised this discomforting question about personal desire. He posed the question to a man who had lived on the edge of healing for thirty-eight years (John 5:5–6). Afflicted by an inability to walk, this fellow fluctuated between reflection and anticipation, memory and hope. He participated in the present only minimally. Habitually, he looked to the past with regrets and to the future with good wishes. He mused about the many times he had just missed an opportunity for healing as he projected the possibility that one day healing would happen.

Jesus asked, "Do you want to get well?" Compassion, not cruelty, suffused the question. By raising the issue of will, Jesus sought to release this man from his bondage to the past and to the future in order to free him to cope with the present. Healing could occur immediately. But healing required risk and effort. Was the man willing to endure the pain of getting well? Remaining crippled might be easier.

Jesus intended to establish reality by way of this question. The lame man faced two options—either continue his pattern of complaints and expectations or accept the requirements involved in getting well. He had to choose between remaining in a bad situation or taking action to make life better. The nature of his will was the crucial factor in his decision.

Jesus' question implicitly declared, Either get up and get on with life or stay sick. Thirty-eight years is long enough. But it looks like you could continue in this intermediate state for another thirty-eight years, so decide right now whether to get up and get well or remain crippled.

You may resent answering some of the questions essential to helpful self-interrogation amid your difficulties. They may sound insensitive or even cruel. But each inquiry serves as a stepping-stone on the path to honesty, functions as a prerequisite for coping with a crisis successfully. Consider:

> Do I complain about my situation as a substitute for doing anything to improve it?
> Am I finding a strange form of satisfaction in my depression?
> Are my continued difficulties providing me with an acceptable excuse for ignoring responsibility?
> Am I enjoying the attention of helpful people so much that getting better no longer seems important?
> Do I get "high" from being "low"?
> Am I holding on to my pain (substitute *grief, anger, disappointment,* or whatever) because I do not want to lose touch completely with the relationship that caused it?
> Do regretting the past and hoping for a better future seem easier than acting to improve my condition in the present?

All these questions are variations of the inquiry inspired by Jesus, "Do you want to get well?" Only you can answer. And only you will know whether or not your answer is truthful. But if you are serious about coping with your present crisis, you must establish reality regarding the nature of your will.

Coping with a crisis demands complete honesty about the crisis. You have to be honest about yourself and the situation you face. Reality, not fantasy, forms the context of authentic hope. Truth equips as well as frees.

Be honest about your situation.

CHAPTER TWO

Get Plenty of Rest

Normally we react to a negative situation by asking immediately, "What can I do?" The urgency of our need to "do something" increases with the severity of the crisis at hand.

Unfortunately, a preoccupation with taking action prolongs or worsens many problems rather than facilitating a quick solution to them. Heightened activity may well increase stress and deepen depression. That combination, in turn, causes incredible fatigue. At the very time you initiate a series of nonstop activities, you experience dragging feet and a sagging spirit. One victim of sustained stress offers a telling confession: "In time of crisis I am much more afraid of my body and emotional symptoms than the actual crisis itself."[1]

Fatigue claims an importance that transcends a concern for physical health alone. Weariness blunts moral sensitivity and negatively impacts ethical decision-making. Controlled experiments have produced irrefutable evidence that differences in the actions of like-minded people confronted by an identical moral challenge relate directly to the varying degrees of fatigue among those people. Rested individuals tend to be more ethically perceptive than persons who are tired. Amid crises especially, rest is essential, both for physical and moral reasons.

Long ago, the renowned counselor Wayne Oates taught me the unshakable truth that the human body will find rest one way or another. We can choose rest as an integral component in our coping with problems, or rest will force itself upon us. Oates interprets Psalm 23:2 literally—God "*makes* me lie down in green pastures."

At first glance, compliance with counsel to rest may appear as the easiest of all the coping responses suggested in this book. Experience tells a different tale, though. Benefiting from times of rest requires resolute intentions and disciplined actions aimed at claiming periods for relaxation.

Dismiss Destructive Myths

Innumerable myths perpetuate a destructive perspective on rest. Constantly staving off the multiple assaults on personhood that are inherent in crises wears us down and makes us vulnerable to the lure of these lies. When internalized, these blatant untruths breed behavior destined to worsen, rather than improve, our troubled situations.

Harmful myths find a ready acceptance among hurting people. They justify postponing honest confrontations with reality and boost severely battered egos. Keep in mind, though, that lasting help comes only from truth. Lies about rest pack a power that hurts all those who accept them.

From the world of business comes a myth that inevitably leads its believers into distress. "Success is worth whatever it costs."

Mouthing some such senseless phrase, scores of troubled people ignore their need for rest and vow to keep going to get a job done, to file a report, to meet a deadline, or to please a particular executive. All of them fail! They fail in their attempts to deny the necessity of rest, and they fail in their professional tasks—ultimately, if not immediately. A mass of personal casualties argues this point much better than any collection of words.

Workplaces provide laborers no reprieve from their personal problems. No professional task enables an individual to defy the energy drain prompted by coping with a crisis, be it public or private in nature.

Grief intensifies a need for rest. Ignoring that truth invites emotional illness. Anxiety exacts sizable expenditures of energy. Refusing to replenish strength destroys the capacity to function responsibly. Seeking to correct overwork by more work makes less sense than trying to extinguish a fire by dousing it with gasoline.

A simple question yields information that offers the best antidote to this business-based myth of success. Ask, "What is success?" Does the word "success" fit a situation in which a job has been completed at the expense of shattered relationships, wrecked emotions, and an abused body? The possibility of a positive answer to that inquiry rests only in a mentality like that expressed by the military strategist who explained, "We had to destroy the village to save it."

"Success" better applies to a situation in which a crisis-beleaguered person recognizes his or her limitations and requests time off from professional responsibilities.

People in difficult situations give voice to a common assumption: "Ready or not, I've got to go to work. My job won't wait." Everybody understands. Economic necessities tied to the demands of the workplace weigh heavily on us all. Unfortunately, not everyone holds a similar appreciation of our need for work-free moments. A wisdom that gives direction to effective coping inspires troubled persons to make a declaration about rest that parallels comments about work. "Like it or not, I've got to have time to rest. My mind, body, and emotions will not wait until I have nothing else to do but rest."

A culture fascinated with macho personalities condones the "super hero" or "super heroine" myth. This lie falls into the same category as that of several pieces of ridiculous counsel passed off as valuable advice: "Big boys don't cry," "Brave girls don't show hurt," "Real men don't need rest," "A good woman remains a tower of strength within her family regardless of how she feels," "Taking time off to face a difficulty is a wimpish cop-out."

Lies. They are all lies. Don't believe them.

Any expectation or suggestion that requires you to be more

than human merits immediate, enthusiastic rejection. No one can be strong all the time. Everyone needs rest and periods of renewal, especially in problem situations. Attempting to transcend your limits as a human being and do what cannot be done destroys your ability to accomplish what is possible within those limits.

Images of super heroes and super heroines properly belong in comic books and cartoons. Neither is a place of honor to which you should aspire.

Destructive advice offered as the product of religious convictions really stirs up trouble. Spiritually supported myths inflict pain more quickly than do their secular counterparts. Two assertions make the point: "You are called to serve other people regardless of your condition" and "If your faith is strong, your capacity for service will know no limitations." When believed, each lie creates guilt in persons who desire rest and labels recreational retreats as symptoms of spiritual failure.

For years I revered an observation from an English cleric of another century. In response to warnings about fatigue, the danger of burning the candle at both ends, he remarked, "What is a candle for but to burn?" The comment struck me as a dramatic statement of an enviable piety—service at all costs, full speed ahead. In more recent days I have seen and experienced the fallacy of such thought. Crazy behavior is not a sure sign of religious stature. A reckless disregard for physical and emotional needs does not create spiritual giants. Irresponsible expenditures of energy fail to exhibit more holiness than responsible investments of time and talents.

Facing a crisis with a commitment that places service to others over taking care of yourself, prizing exhaustion over rest, fails to qualify as an admirable religious approach to life. Christianity challenges such thought rather than commends it.

Traditionally, the term "messianic complex" has been used to expose the fallacious thought of persons who assume they carry the weight of the world on their shoulders and hold the redemption of the world in their hands. Stereotypically, people who possess this mentality wear themselves out trying to solve everyone else's problems, to care for the hurts of scores of acquaintances, and to keep all their family members and friends happy. How could Jesus inspire such rank delusions of grandeur in anybody?

Take another look at the idea of a messianic complex. A careful examination of the life of Jesus gives new and more positive meaning to the messianic model. To live like the Messiah involves taking regular retreats from activities (even from the lofty work of healing and saving) for purposes of rest, relaxation, and recuperation. Strict adherence to the lifestyle of Jesus requires facing crises with a strong resolve to take care of your own physical, emotional, and spiritual needs.

Perhaps the singular most damaging myth commending a disregard for rest involves the idea of "personal exception." Evidence of an acceptance of this lie emerges in numerous common expressions: "I know the value of rest, but I also know my capacity for work. I don't require the kind of rest needed by other people." Or, "Sure, I'm well aware of precautionary actions to take when facing problems. But my problems are different, and I have coping abilities most people do not possess. I have neither a need nor an intention to rest."

Some myths have a basis in fact. Not this one. A direct, nondebatable, irrefutable relationship exists between effective coping and responsible resting. No exceptions! A disdain for that reality sets the stage for tragedy.

Disregard Poisonous Praise

How can praise be poisonous? Easy. It happens all the time.

Everybody needs affirmation and acceptance from other people. In times of crisis and situations of hurt, those common needs take on outlandish importance. Individuals develop a hyper eagerness to experience the approval of others. Discretion and discernment diminish. At that point, comments laced with poison can be heard as words of encouragement and support. An uncritical acceptance of statements that sound like help give rise to more hurt.

A man immersed in grief over the loss of a child and desperately in need of time away from his job stops short of requesting a vacation after listening to a supervisor. The well-meaning leader says to his employee, "We admire your faithfulness to the company during this difficult time. You continue to do the work of three people and never complain. You are quite a man." The grief-stricken fellow knows better. I'm weak and need help, he thinks to himself. But fearing that an honest confession of his condition will jeopardize more affirmation, he says nothing. He aches for affirmation. This man is literally dying for praise.

Drawing from a cultural litany of praise dedicated to strength, success, and overwork, well-intentioned people express admiration for destructive lifestyles. Believe me. I myself have been suckered by lethal encouragement.

"We appreciate the long hours you work, though we don't know how you do it. You keep going when the rest of us have to stop. You exemplify commitment to service." As the woman spoke to me, I thought, If you only knew! I can barely lift my feet to walk. And I don't even like what I'm doing. But I flashed a gracious smile and remained quiet. My struggle with a critical situation had created an insatiable need for commendation. In this way, comments intended as honest praise encourage a pattern of behavior sure to result in physical illness and emotional hurt.

Disregard all statements that tempt you to fake a strength you do not possess, to accept more work when an overload already exists, and to keep going though everything within you is crying "Stop!" At this point, motivations do not really matter. Well-meaning people often encourage suicidal behavior. Unfortunately, their good intentions do not alter the devastation you experience. You can die (professionally or emotionally, and maybe even literally), seeking to receive or justify affirmation from sincere people who wish you well.

Life-giving praise seems more difficult to find. If you do not hear it from others, offer it to yourself. Reach deep inside and call up self-affirmation. Keep in mind that admitting weakness takes real strength. Knowing when to say "Enough!" indicates authentic wisdom. Deciding to stop for rest represents a courage capable of sustaining health. Confessing hurt and requesting help model the kind of integrity that enhances the quality of life for a person, a fellowship, or a corporation.

Spend Time Outdoors

Staying indoors for long periods of time can shrink your world and dull your sensitivities. Of course, if you have an illness that mandates confinement or a disability that prohibits enjoying the out-of-doors, remaining inside represents your way to health. If not, though, moving about outside your place of residence can tremendously enhance your capacity for coping with troublesome developments in your life.

Problem-burdened people often give multiple valid-sounding reasons for staying inside their homes. An affinity for the comfort and security of lounging amid familiar surroundings produces statements such as "I just don't feel like getting out," "I'm too tired to take a walk," or "I'm afraid I'll catch a cold if I spend time outside." Then, too, taking care of compelling responsibilities can always win out over activities devoted to personal pleasure: "I have to pay these bills" or "I'm expecting an important phone call that I cannot afford to miss."

If at all possible, resist temptations to remain inside. Spend some time outdoors everyday. In addition to experiencing a unique quality of rest, your coping abilities will be enhanced.

A brief, quick walk around your neighborhood can expand your horizons and deliver you from a preoccupation with your problems. Down the street you notice a FOR SALE sign in the front yard of a longtime resident and muse, "I wonder what is happening in their lives." Watching a little girl steer her wobbly two-wheeler along the sidewalk, you smile as you think, She wants so badly to ride her bike without training wheels. On the other side of the street you see a young mother pushing a stroller with twins in it. Fascinated by the look of awe on their faces, you forget momentarily the stack of unpaid bills on your dining room table.

During a bad stretch of time in my life, I resisted leaving my house for almost any reason. Family members and friends encouraged me to try brief walks in the neighborhood. After a long series of refusals, one day, for some unexplainable reason, I made myself amble around outside for a while. Immediately (literally right then), I discovered a freshness in feelings, a clarity of thought, and a liveliness in emotions that had been absent for months. No longer do I have to make myself embark on a daily trek around our neighborhood. I look forward to it.

God's good gifts dominate nature. But only by venturing out-of-doors do we see them and find delight in them. During almost every one of my outings I stumble upon a surprise, experience a moment of unexpected pleasure, catch a glimpse of breathtaking beauty, or find myself fascinated by some earthly creature. Diversion, relaxation, and even renewal result from discovering a yellow daffodil protruding from a snowdrift in early spring, studying the subtle blend of pinks and whites in a fully opened cherry blossom, or feeling a cool blast of autumn wind that sends red, gold, and orange leaves flying.

If mobility presents a problem for you, perhaps you can regularly sit out-of-doors. An amazing array of activities and an expansive cross section of creation can be viewed from a stationary position in a yard or on a porch. Sitting and absorbing what is going on around you can be relaxing, enjoyable, and enlightening. This is rest in its best sense.

After spending time outdoors, you will return indoors not only more rested but with a renewed awareness of God's continuing activity in creation. Equally important, what you have seen of God's handiwork in the world may fill you with an exciting hunch that God can still do something good, in your life and with your life.

Exercise Your Body

Physical exercise usually aids rest. Double-talk? No. Troubled people commonly find that sitting comfortably or lying down peacefully is much easier after a period of energy-expending activities.

A person bothered by swirling emotions and knotted muscles benefits immensely from a brisk physical workout. Do not be intimidated by thoughts of gymnastic heroics. Invaluable help can be derived from simple activities—a brief walk, limited jogging, back bends, push-ups, or other muscle-stretching exercises.

Feelings can trick you. Often we do not feel like doing precisely what we most need to do to feel better. Amazingly, a reasonable amount of exercise even when you think you are too tired to try it can replace an oppressive sense of fatigue with a restful sense of fulfillment. At least it works that way for me. During especially difficult times, my daily walk-run helps relieve stress in my shoulders, ease tension in my head, remove anxiety in my stomach, and lift heaviness from my spirit. Exercise makes quality rest possible.

Relax Your Mind

To cope responsibly with a crisis, observe an occasional moratorium on analysis, investigation, and reflection. A weary mind needs rest every bit as much as a tired body.

Think what happens after you stare at a set of parallel lines or a collection of dots for an extended period of time. If you do not rest your eyes, the lines seem to run together or the dots become a massive blur. A similar phenomenon plagues a mind that studies a problem without rest. Dullness, confusion, and intellectual blindness accompany the mental fatigue that develops. Thoughts become counterproductive as you lose a healthy perspective on your difficulties. Any possibility of good decision-making diminishes dramatically.

Do not hesitate to make use of aids to mental relaxation. Numerous audio and video cassettes have been produced for this specific purpose. Reading an entertaining book, cheering during a sporting event, watching a good movie, or listening to enjoyable music also helps bring rest to the mind.

"But I feel guilty thinking of anything else. This problem deserves all my attention," many people declare. Examine such declarations realistically. True guilt stems from wrongdoing, violations of ethical norms, and betrayals of conscience. Resting the mind represents obedience to the divine will as well as conformity to the laws of mental health. Guilt prompted by claiming a period for much-needed rest should be ignored, if not negated.

Mental relaxation while coping with a crisis mirrors the importance of physical recuperation when running a week-long cross-country race. You cannot cope with the challenges confronting you without meaningful periods of mental rest.

Give yourself permission to rest your mind. And then enjoy it.

Keep a Full Calendar

That's right. You read the words correctly: Keep a full calendar. Read on. I have anticipated your reactions to this suggestion: "That counsel does not make sense. How can adding more engagements to your calendar, much less staying booked up, contribute to rest? I get tired just thinking about it." Allow me to explain.

Most people assume that entries into their date books reflect responsibilities to other people—"Attend a committee meeting

GET PLENTY OF REST

at the church," "Make phone calls for the blood drive," "Conduct a staff conference." Only times spent with professionals are considered exceptions to this general rule—"Go to the doctor for an annual physical," "Get a haircut." In this approach to scheduling, individuals search for blocks of unplanned time with hopes of seeing a movie, attending a ball game, or taking a nap. They reserve rest and relaxation for the "leftovers," the undesignated hours, on their calendars. This plan for getting rest does not work. It is fatally flawed from its inception.

With calendar in hand, consider a totally different means of planning your time. Schedule blocks of time for yourself as well as for other people. No rules prohibit it. An interest in good health and responsible coping with problems dictates it. Not all the entries in your appointment book have to involve expenditures of your energy.

Do advance planning for rest—whether restful activities or total inactivity—just as you do for work. Refuse to settle for only the rest that can be worked into leftover moments. Plan for times of rest and reserve those times on your calendar as hard-and-fast appointments. Then honor those engagements with the same intensity of commitment that you devote to conferences with your boss, meetings with your best customer, or visits with your accountant. If someone requests your presence or your services during one of these periods scheduled for rest, say, "I already have an engagement for that time that I can't break." Hold moments set aside for yourself as inviolately as you do times devoted to others.

Occasionally a woman indicates to me that she feels guilty telling someone she has an appointment when the time is designated "only" for herself. Such guilt springs from insecurity, from a lack of self-esteem, or, most likely, from an inadequate respect for personal needs. A more appropriate guilt stems from failing to protect times for personal re-creation.

Taking care of yourself, finding time for rest, is a spiritual responsibility as old as the first stories of creation and as basic as the earliest collections of religious law. Failing to take care of yourself under the guise of selflessness qualifies as an error every bit as severe as rank selfishness.

Fill up your calendar by making certain that times for rest are scheduled and kept.

Let Go

But how do you do it? The physical rest, the mental rest, any of it? Even if the time has been scheduled and an opportunity for rest is available, how do you find rest with your emotions on edge, anxieties sky high, adrenaline pumping, and mind racing? How can anyone rest when facing a situation fraught with devastating implications?

A sense of security may be the key. (Perhaps that is another name for faith.) An ability to turn loose, to relax, relates directly to the answers you give to severe security-related inquiries: For what am I responsible in this crisis? To whom am I accountable? Finding peace in answering these questions creates the possibility of rest.

In dealing with problems, times come when we have to admit that we have done all we can do to correct wrongs, alleviate hurt, and build a foundation for future action. At that point, waiting becomes a necessity. As difficult as it is, we have to wait for time to pass, for the natural processes of healing to occur, for therapy to yield its benefits, or for someone else to do something we cannot do. God knows, such waiting is hard.

Acknowledging God's involvement in our waiting encourages a security that sustains patience. The divine truth of "in the fullness of time" comforts us with its certainty even as it challenges us with its ambiguity.

The health and stability of what resides inside us influence most the manner in which we cope with what goes on around us. Confrontations with life at its worst demand that we be at our best. That requires rest.

Rest is a physical and mental necessity and a moral responsibility. Claim rest as a source of enjoyment if at all possible. If not, accept it as a non-negotiable discipline.

Get plenty of rest.

CHAPTER THREE

Reach Out to Friends

A time of crisis is a time for companionship. Unfortunately, many people overlook this vital truth. Consequently, they suffer more than necessary.

Confronted by major difficulties, you will be tempted to withdraw into a shell, to repress all your concerns deep inside yourself, and to refuse to interact with others about the problems that plague your life. Shame, embarrassment, or grief—each a common ingredient in a crisis—strengthens the lure of solitude tremendously. Resist these temptations with all your might. Giving in to your desires will rob you of fulfillment for a fundamental need. In a time of crisis you need your friends.

No one can bear everything alone. Macho myths to the contrary, everybody needs friendship generally, if not a specific form of assistance, from someone else. Given a crisis situation, your ordinary need for friends increases inestimably.

The results from two research projects are instructive. In one, seven thousand people who had suffered a cataclysmic disease were surveyed. One conclusion drawn from the findings of that survey stands out. Individuals who enjoyed a strong support system of friends and family members survived at a much higher rate than those without such support.[1]

In the second, after extensive studies, an authority on stress wrote, "In my experience, no person who has gone to pieces, lost his or her self-esteem, and then found a firm place on which to stand did so without being loved greatly by someone—someone who had enough faith and confidence in that person to help in his or her recovering a sense of worth as a human being."[2]

Ironically, people who work in the helping professions

often exhibit the most reticence to seek help from others when caught up in difficulties. Deceptive assumptions lead to destructive consequences: "I know how to get through this on my own. I have helped scores of people through similar situations; surely I can get myself through this one." No way! Persons who regularly help others do not become self-sufficient supermen and superwomen in the process. When plagued by problems, even helpers need help.

Troubled people need friends. All troubled people.

Stay Away from People Who Hurt You

I know a man who wears his feelings on his sleeve. When we talk after he has a bad day, I know it right away. If I share a personal problem with him, even when all is well in his world, he becomes absorbed in my difficulty to the point that he cannot help. On several occasions I have been in a good mood when I began a conversation with this person, only to feel that I was in a pit at the conclusion of our dialogue. This makes no sense. I no longer talk to this man frequently. If I am troubled, I do not talk to him at all. I continue to like him and appreciate many of the activities we enjoy together. But I refuse to hand over to this fellow thoughts and ideas with which he can unintentionally hurt me.

You know people like that. Admit it. Identify them.

You would not deliberately walk into the path of a rattlesnake poised to strike you with poisonous venom or stroll unprotected into a swarm of bees ready to sting you. Neither should you subject yourself to people who invariably harm you. Avoid them. Especially when you are trying to cope with a crisis, stay away from folks who hurt you and turn to friends who nurture you.

Watch out particularly for people who claim to know your problems and state their desire to offer conditional help. Usually, they do not know nearly as much as they claim, and they will deliver only a minimal amount of help, if any at all.

Recently a young man described to me the pain he continues to experience because of a situation in which he was made the victim of malicious gossip. As his crisis unfolded, he received well over three hundred letters of concern. Almost every piece of correspondence he read contained statements of conditional support: "I will be glad to help you if you are innocent, as I surmise you are." "Count on our assistance after you have been vindicated by the appropriate authorities." Only two letter writers offered this fellow unconditional help: "I don't believe the gossip I hear. However, neither your guilt nor your innocence is a factor in my offer to support you and help you."

No doubt you have been the recipient of similar comments: "I will be glad to help you as soon as these ridiculous charges against you have been cleared up"; "I want to get with you after you have worked through your grief"; "You have my support and you can count on my demonstrating it once public sentiments change a bit for the better." This is not help! Remarks like these portray speakers more concerned for themselves than for you. Recognize the true nature of what is being said to you.

Help, genuine help, comes from people who care for you. Such folks do not have to know all about your problem before assisting you in dealing with it. People who really care for you do not make their help contingent on revelations of guilt or innocence if there is a question about either.

Conditional help, actually a serious misnomer, creates a potential for more hurt. Stay away from people who offer assistance with strings attached. Very likely, their agenda aims more at judging and controlling you than helping you.

You need real help. Much like grace, authentic help arrives as a gift of love unaltered by presumptions or even revelations of wrongdoing. That is what you need. You already have enough troubles. Don't expose yourself to the possibility of more. Seek out caring friends. Go where help is available.

Share Your Story Selectively

You will want to talk about your crisis, eventually if not immediately. Regular sessions with a professional therapist can help immensely. However, these formal consultations probably will not satisfy your desire to unburden your soul to sympathetic friends. You will long for discussions with someone you can count on to listen with compassion and understanding, someone who will readily agree to help carry the weight of your burden.

In the throes of a crisis you may sense that everyone else is talking about your difficulties (often an untrue assumption). That perception, whether accurate or inaccurate, usually brings about a resolve to speak for yourself. Be careful. You can easily overdo it.

You do need to speak with friends about your situation. But be selective. First, be selective in what you say. Second, be selective in choosing to whom you say it.

Most all your friends want to know how you are doing. Tell them. Many of your friends will ask, "What happened? What's the story?" In response to these questions, exercise caution. For people whom you judge to be genuinely interested, sketch the broad parameters of your crisis. However, do not relate the whole story in minute detail to everyone who inquires about it. Such efforts will exhaust you personally and only minimally benefit your friends.

As a general rule, you do best to relate the details of your experience to only one person outside your family—at most, two (not counting professional counselors). What you have to tell (about what troubles you, what you need to share, what you want understood) is *your* story. It does not belong to the community. Find one person whose confidentiality you trust, whose interest in you is without question, and unburden yourself only to that person.

Do not forfeit your right to privacy. Every crisis involves

information that will be handled insensitively at best and, at worst, misunderstood, mishandled, or even badly distorted if it becomes public property. Every community contains people who thrive on bandying about stories of other folks' pain. Do not make public disclosures of reflections that belong in private.

"What if there are rumors?" you ask. "What if lies are being told? What if my problem is being misrepresented?" Count on it. Assume the likelihood of these developments, and recognize that you cannot do anything about them.

Attempts to track down the source of every piece of false information about your situation for purposes of correction are worthless. You will only wear yourself out and thus weaken your ability to cope. True friends will be unswayed by gossip, your enemies will believe the worst, and those people who delight in spreading rumors will be undeterred by facts.

At some point in the coping process, you may have to check a tendency to talk about your difficulties with everyone you meet. Images come to mind. A recently divorced friend is preoccupied with her pain. At every opportunity, oblivious to the nature of the occasion, she accosts people with a bitter harangue about her former husband. I know a father gridlocked in grief. In every conversation (with anyone about anything), he finds a way to direct attention toward the problem of his son's drug addiction.

What happens is perfectly understandable. You devote yourself to the demands of a threatening crisis day after day. Work on that crisis becomes all-consuming. The extent of your problem gradually becomes the boundary of your world. So naturally you assume that everybody has as much interest in your difficulties as you do. Your pain tops the list of subjects you want to discuss in all conversations. Understandable, yes. But your assumption must be challenged and the temptation to have a single focus in every social interaction rejected.

Not everyone wants to hear about your problems every time they see you. Even the people closest to you do not want to listen to a monologue on your coping success or failure each time you are together. That does not mean they have ceased to care for you. Sometimes your friends need to talk rather than listen. Occasionally they get to a point where they just cannot deal with your difficulties. Besides, you need the discipline of contributing to conversations that do not revolve around you.

Telling your story is extremely important. But telling your story selectively may be even more important.

Tell Your Friends What You Need

Friends cognizant of your troubles usually inquire, "Is there anything I can do to help?" Take that question seriously. Answer it specifically. Your friends will know how best to help you only if you tell them.

What if I don't know what I need? you think. This is very possible, especially early in a crisis. Shock, hurt, confusion, and pain can dull your sensitivities to the point that you do not even know what to ask for.

Begin here. You share at least four needs with all people who struggle with crises. Speak to your friends about these needs.

Acceptance. Persons caught up in (or beaten down by) a crisis need acceptance. A woman whose job has been terminated senses a level of rejection that goes far beyond unemployment. A man battling a serious disease assumes that people would prefer not to have him around. Beset by grief, a woman views herself as a downer, a wet blanket, a miserable person who makes other people uncomfortable. Publicly embarrassed by his poor judgment, a man decides he must endure social ostracism as part of his punishment.

You need acceptance, normal acceptance. Counterfeits do not help. Subterfuge hurts. Superficial affirmations and condescending statements of concern strike you like poison-tipped arrows shot into your heart. You need genuine acceptance.

Whether aware of your condition or not, you want to be viewed, heard, treated, and accepted just like everybody else, not as someone special because of your trouble. Badgered by difficulties, an abnormal need develops for normal acceptance. You can spot the real thing instantly. People convey genuine acceptance by attitudes, words, invitations, assignments, and contacts.

If you feel unaccepted by your friends (or unacceptable to them), let them know it. You may have to explain yourself. "I need you to treat me like you did before all these troubles began. I appreciate your interest in my problem, but sometimes I have to talk about something else. Tell me a joke. Gripe about your work. Tell me about the ball game. I want you to care for me because of who I am as a person, not because I am someone facing a crisis."

Friends are not always sure how to react to you when they see you hurting. They may assume it best to pull back, to give you space, to treat you as fragile. You can tell real friends about real needs. If your friends do not take helpful initiatives, feel free to say to them, "Let's go to a movie." "Could we have dinner together?" or "I need a hug." They will appreciate your candor. You will appreciate their acceptance.

Contact. After being clobbered by a crisis, you may think you want to be left alone. That's certainly understandable. People have hurt you: deserted you, betrayed you, lied to you, attacked you, scandalized you, rejected you. Naturally you fear contact. You don't want to be hurt anymore.

Thoughts of interacting even with friends raise anxieties. "Will they ask me disturbing questions? Will I have to talk about myself? What if I see them attempting to disguise their disapproval of me or their disgust with me? I can't stand one more person evaluating my condition and telling me what I ought to do. I don't ever want to hear again that critical, paternalistic tone of voice."

You may not need long visits from friends, but you do need contacts with them. Brief phone calls from people who care or handwritten notes received through the mail can help you immensely.

When you do spend an extended period of time with people you appreciate, you may find it most helpful if the agenda directs attention away from the personal concerns of anyone present. Getting together for dessert, to watch a televised ball game, or to walk through a mall offers a splendid way to enjoy contact with other folks.

When a crisis continues for a prolonged period of time and troubles persist relentlessly, you may worry that your friends will forget you. Occasional contacts from friends negate that fear. If friends fail to call you, however, call them.

Help. A starving child needs food. A drowning man needs a life jacket. A sunburned woman needs a cooling, healing salve. Some things are obvious. If you are in trouble, you need help from your friends.

"Most of my needs are so apparent that if my friends don't pick up on them by observation they will probably not be sensitive enough to help me even if I make a suggestion," you tell yourself. Be careful here. Your needs dominate your attention, inviting your constant thought. Not so with your friends. They think about their own needs, responsibilities, and jobs. Your friends' failure to recognize your needs readily in no way indicates insensitivity or an unwillingness to help.

You probably do not face a crisis involving starvation, drowning, or severe sunburn. Most likely, your situation is much less obvious and far more complex than any of those difficulties. Thus, you cannot assume that the forms of help you need will be recognized quickly even by those who know you best. To get the help you need, you will have to ask for it.

Be specific: "Will you please write a letter recommending me for that job?" "Do you mind helping me go through these insurance papers so I can establish how much money I owe the hospital?" "I would appreciate your including me in a dinner party sometime when those present will not try to interrogate me about my divorce or set me up with a blind date." "Will you call a few of our mutual friends and let them know I need to hear from them?"

Do not hesitate to ask your friends for help. But give them time to respond to your request. And allow them the right to say they cannot do what you ask.

Honesty. Honesty from your friends carries an importance equal to that of honesty with yourself. It is also equally problematic.

Caring friends do not want to add to your pain. Thus they often do not challenge your system of denial, correct your inaccurate judgments, or tell you just how rough the road ahead will actually be. They surmise that they are doing you a favor. They are not. When non-confrontational friends allow your harmful illusions to persist and affirm your distorted view of reality as the foundation upon which to put life back together, their good intentions lead to hurt they are unable to prevent.

Ask your friends to be honest with you. Encourage them to speak the truth in love. Prod them for such talk if you must. Invite honesty from your friends by being honest with them. "Please level with me. I may not want to hear the truth as you see it, but I need to hear it. Even if the truth hurts, you will help me by keeping me in touch with reality. I can separate liking you from not liking what you say to me."

Honesty from your friends, even when discomforting, can serve as an important source of security. Life may be in a tailspin. You may be dizzied by disasters. But you know you can count on insights from your friends and trust what they say.

Keep Your Relationships in Focus

Coping with a crisis exacts a heavy toll. Energy diminishes. Reasoning skills weaken. Emotions become frayed. Extreme vulnerability develops, a predictable condition that requires no apology but demands attention.

A friend may not know the perils of your predicament as

REACH OUT TO FRIENDS

well as you do. At this point, supported by your friends, you may need to reach beyond them for sources of help. A professional therapist can quickly point out the dangers inherent in your situation.

Guard against the development of an unhealthy dependency on your friends. This problem can emerge almost imperceptibly. With great appreciation for a friend's assistance, you may subtly cast that person in the role of one of your parents or of your spouse. Unrealistic expectations develop. Eventually you may allow help from such friends to replace all efforts to help yourself. Then you will refuse to see successes and failures as your responsibility. You praise your friends when things go well. You blame your friends if anything goes wrong. Such dependency destroys coping skills.

Another danger to be avoided in relation to friends stems from confusing supportive compassion with romantic emotions. Combine your state of extreme vulnerability with your overwhelming need for loving acceptance and you create a situation fraught with potential problems. A phone call, an embrace, or an encouraging visit from a caring friend can be misunderstood.

With your self-confidence virtually destroyed, the concern of a friend buoys your spirit. With your self-esteem in shambles, you long to feel wanted or needed. Any hint of a satisfying relationship stimulates an interest sustained by reasoning, "I cannot get enough love." In such a situation, kindness from a friend can seem like romance. Sensitivity may take on overtones of sexuality. You begin to surmise: "I believe he has more than a normal interest in me," or "I wonder what she meant by saying, 'You know I love you,' " or "Maybe he wants to share in my life more intimately."

You may not be able to avoid such confusion. Worse still, you may begin to sense "an undeniable new love" catapulting you toward "an inevitable union." Rational arguments to the contrary will not help you. However, you can resolve to pursue neither your thoughts nor your feelings until you have consulted a professional who can help you clarify what is happening. You owe that to "your new love" and to yourself.

Both dependency and romance in relation to your friends worsen your plight. The crisis that caused you to reach out to your friends remains. And a hundred more difficulties rush toward you like storm clouds swept by gale-force winds.

Beware. Clarify the nature of your relationships with friends.

View Friends Realistically and Expect Disappointments

At times friends will disappoint you. Not because they cease to care for you, not because they don't want to help you, they simply have more to do than work on your problems. You know that truth (and understand it) intellectually. But emotionally you struggle with it.

Extended unemployment produces panic. Prolonged grief creates despair. Relentless anxiety destroys patience. Pounded by such problems, you reach a point of desperation.

After a needs-oriented conversation, a friend casually remarks, "I will call my CEO buddy about you," or "I want to talk to the doctor on your behalf," or "I will give you a book that has proven a godsend for many people mourning a loss." Then, getting ready to leave, he says, "I will be in touch soon." Propelled by your desperation, you leap at his words like reaching for a life jacket on a sinking ship and clutch them as a sign of hope. An internal clock starts ticking. Eagerly you wait for it to strike. Every morning begins with the question, "Will I hear from my friend today?" Your friend has no idea of the profound expectations his off-the-cuff comment engendered in you. He gets busy with other things. You never get a report from him. The next time you see him, he makes no mention of the promises from the previous conversation.

No maliciousness is involved. Your friend has no intention

of ignoring you or hurting you. Either he forgot his casual remarks; or he tried to act on them and, when unsuccessful at first, allowed them to slip his mind; or he suddenly found himself besieged by a series of family or work-related crises in his own life.

Inevitably, disappointment develops. Keep in mind, though, that not even your most sensitive friends can fathom the groping-for-life intensity of your concerns. What you wrestle with every waking hour of every day, your friends think about most seriously only when they are with you and work on only as their time allows.

Reach out to your friends. Accept graciously what they can provide in the way of help. But don't count on them to become miracle workers. Even your closest friends will not be able to do for you all they intend (and maybe promise) to do, much less all you want them to do. But they remain your friends. And their gift of a caring relationship has value beyond measure.

Friends and acquaintances differ. Crises usually establish that distinction dramatically. Individuals with whom you have shared innumerable experiences when all was well never even call when your life tumbles in. People you thought to be good friends offer no support whatsoever. But other individuals, whose interest and help you did not expect, become sources of constant encouragement. Troubles serve as a truth serum when it comes to clarifying the quality of your various interpersonal relationships.

You probably have many acquaintances. Chances are you have only a few friends. One can be terrific. Two or three represent relational affluence.

A now-deceased friend of mine once observed, "A friend is someone who listens to your song and then sings it for you when you no longer can do the singing." He knew. His words were born amid a crisis precipitated by a brain tumor. And he was right.

A friend is a person you view with reverence but with whom

you never hesitate to be irreverent.[3] In the presence of a friend, you can unload. Unwind. With friends you feel free to share your burdens, voice your anger, try to describe your despair. Friends laugh together. And cry.

A friend functions as an instrument of grace—believing in you (maybe with more confidence than you believe in yourself), offering you forgiveness before you request it (if forgiveness is needed), and instilling hope. When blessed by a grace-filled visit from a friend, you actually feel better, physically and emotionally. Delighting in time spent with a friend, you understand the meaning of Jacob's comment to Esau, "To see your face is like seeing the face of God" (Gen. 33:10).

When trying to cope with a crisis, resist all tendencies to pull away from people who care for you. Allow them to reach out to you. Reach out to them.

Reach out to friends.

CHAPTER FOUR

Fight Cynicism

Attitude affects coping like few other factors. A healthy outlook on life contributes to effective coping amid a crisis. Conversely, a bad attitude not only prevents positive developments in dealing with problems but often worsens a crisis significantly. Sometimes a near-crippling sickness ensues.

More and more formal studies support conventional wisdom's affirmation of the importance of a positive personal attitude. Similarly, clinical experiments and well publicized social incidents document the destructive power of a negative perspective.

A few years ago a fascinating series of events at Monterrey Park football stadium in California received a great deal of media attention.[1] During a high school football game, some of the spectators became ill with symptoms of food poisoning. The physician who examined these people discovered one commonality among them. Each of the sickened persons had consumed a particular soft drink dispensed by machines under the stands. Officials suspected the cola syrup was contaminated. Perhaps a dangerous leakage of copper sulfate from the pipes through which the cola was dispensed had polluted people's drinks.

Without waiting for a definite cause of the spectators' illness, and desiring to prevent any further problems, stadium officials announced over the loudspeakers that people should not drink any of the cola dispensed by a certain machine in the concessions stand. Spectators were told that a few people had become ill after drinking this product, and the symptoms of their illness were described.

Immediately, an epidemic of sickness swept through the people in that stadium. Even individuals who had not gone near the vending machine in question bent over double with symptoms of food poisoning. Hundreds of people fled the stands. Many others declared themselves too sick to move. Ambulances from five different hospitals transported people from the football stadium to emergency rooms. Two hundred people were hospitalized.

Amid all this chaos, officials discovered that no problems existed either with the cola syrup or with the machine through which it was dispensed. They were still not certain of the cause of the initial cases of illness, but they knew it was not related to a soft drink. Immediately this word was boomed through the loudspeakers at the stadium. Another astounding development followed.

People suddenly and miraculously recovered from their illnesses. Just as they had been overcome by sickness in a split second, now instantaneously they were well. In both instances, nothing had happened except a public announcement that shaped a dominant attitude among the individuals present. When people thought they were ill (or surmised that they might be ill), they became ill. When these same people were told that no cause for their illness had been found, they recovered. How important is attitude?

Tremendous power resides in a person's attitude—power to hurt and power to help. Amid a crisis, an individual's attitude can make the difference between coping effectively with problems and being hopelessly overcome by them.

When trust breaks down, cynicism—a dangerous attitude—breaks out. Pain keeps it going.

The longer cynicism continues unchecked, the more difficult it becomes to correct. Cynicism covers the soul like plaster of Paris. Early on, the application resembles an easily removable paste; just wipe it off or wash it away. Left to set, though, cynicism hardens into a cast that restricts the freedom of a person's spirit and prevents the circulation of health-giving fresh air.

Guard against cynicism. Prevent it if at all possible. Should prevention fail, work hard to rid yourself of cynicism at the earliest possible moment. If you see that you are losing the battle, seek help.

Successfully coping with a crisis requires fighting cynicism.

Identify the Enemy

A good fighter knows what or whom to engage in battle—the strengths, weaknesses, tendencies, and tactics of the enemy. Dealing a death blow to cynicism necessitates similar insights. Studiously determine specific answers to these questions: "What is causing my cynicism?" and "What must I defeat to overcome the sources, symptoms, and expressions of cynicism in my life?"

Beware of generalizations. Different persons find different answers to each of these inquiries.

A major disappointment or a series of disappointments destroys confidence regarding any promise in life. When a woman receives word that another person was chosen for a job she was sure she would get, her dashed hopes prompt a pervasive cynical perspective that reaches far beyond the realm of employment. Wearing a scowl on her face, she scoffs, "I did everything right, anticipated success, and got drubbed by failure. Competence counts for nothing in this world. Neither do goodness and fairness."

Unrelieved anger gives birth to cynicism. Prolonged rage against a person or persons, a situation, or an institution mushrooms into a radical negativism about all of life. A man badly shaken by his wife's marital infidelity and subsequent demand for a divorce develops an obnoxious defeatist mentality regarding everything of value. "Virtue has no reward. The institution of marriage is a trap. Only fools find anyone to trust," he barks.

Resentment spawns cynicism. Watching other people receive rewards that you feel you rightly deserve but never will enjoy quickly generates negativism and douses all light. A shroud of darkness impairs good vision. Cynicism prevails. A young girl looks on as her best friend is lauded by the media and rewarded with numerous scholarship offers from major universities because of her skills on the tennis court. The onlooker, a straight-A student starved for affirmation and believing herself too poor to pursue a college degree, resents the disparity between the two situations. Cynicism erupts in a conversation with her parents: "What's the use in trying? Society's values are twisted. I might as well give up!"

Hurt hammers away at a healthy attitude. Only exceptionally strong people successfully survive the onslaught. While struggling with pain induced by rejection from a longtime friend, a man undergoes a prolonged period of unrelievable nausea. He sees nothing but hurt around him and feels nothing but discomfort within him. For this fellow, as for almost anyone, relentless agony breeds a defeatist mentality. A friend of mine, a college senior on the eve of graduation, sadly epitomized this situation in these words of personal confession: "Life is like a mouse running through a maze. If you are lucky enough to get to the end of it, you find a small piece of cheese atop a trap. Eat the cheese and you die."

Combinations of these emotions can assault the human spirit with deadly force. Erratic, maybe frantic, biting questions signal a deteriorating emotional situation. "What's the use of trying to do right?" "Who cares how I feel?" Such rhetorical questions admit of only negative responses that reinforce a depressed spirit. Apart from correction, these inquiries soon give way to blunt convictions dropped like bombs: "Life is not fair!" "Whatever bad can happen will happen." A cynic doesn't care that damage may be inflicted on others by such missiles of gloom and doom.

Pay attention to what you say as well as to how you say it. Watch and listen for tipoffs of trouble like these: "Look what a commitment to ethics did to my business. My crooked competi-

FIGHT CYNICISM

tor thrives while I'm filing for bankruptcy." Or, "Don't speak to me about love and loyalty. The man I loved with all my heart treated me worse than most people treat their enemies." Or, "Everybody is just alike—greedy, selfish, concerned only about themselves—Christians included!"

Well-meaning friends and family members can unintentionally worsen your plight. "I understand exactly how you feel," they say. "I don't blame you for thinking like that. If I were you, I wouldn't trust anybody either." They want to help. Accept their empathy gratefully. But do not equate sympathy for your attitude with support for it. Understanding cynicism no more eradicates the problem than understanding a malignancy halts its deadly spread.

Sometimes you need to bite your lip to form a dam to hold back a flood of cynical words. Silence does not do away with cynicism. But it does prevent speech that feeds and entrenches cynical thoughts. Seldom, if ever, should we say all that we think. Nowhere is that general principle more applicable than in relation to openly espousing a negative philosophy of life.

Defeating cynicism is essential to healthy coping. Cynicism sets in motion destructive dynamics. A medical doctor writes, "If you presume that you live in a hostile universe, the reaction to that presumption is what wears out your body."[2] That's not all. The mind and the spirit suffer as well.

Counter with Realism

What weapon most effectively combats cynicism? Not unbridled optimism. Persons programmed to declare in all circumstances, "Life is great; things could be worse; look on the bright side," drive cynics up the wall. Relentless positivism also fails to conquer cynicism. People who paste on smiles, fearing even an appearance of unhappiness, can push an individual into cynicism rather than away from it.

In deference to a good attitude, you cannot afford to say more about life than is true. No virtue exists in calling a bad situation good. Don't confuse a healthy perspective with an ability to claim that you feel great when life falls in on you. That too is sick, every bit as harmful to coping and good health as cynicism.

Realism best counteracts cynicism—a thoroughgoing realism. Unfortunately, amid a crisis fraught with overwhelming difficulties, realism can sound like cynicism. But major differences differentiate the two.

A cynic declares, "You can't count on anybody." A realist observes, "You cannot count on anybody else to do for you what you must do for yourself." Similarly, an embittered individual exclaims, "The world is out to get me; all is vanity," while a hurting though enlightened struggler sighs, "Not everyone cares about my troubles. And not all who say they care enough to help do or will. But a few, or maybe only one, will act on the compassion they profess." Realism differs dramatically from cynicism.

Disappointments need not pummel you headlong into despair. Occasionally things turn out right. Be realistic.

Anger at everybody and everything ignores reality. Not everyone is against you. To the contrary, some people care about you more than you imagine. Even in a bad situation, you will discover forms of personal support that legitimately give rise to appreciation and gratitude.

Resentment recedes, if not dissipates completely, when challenged by realism. We may not get all we deserve. Often life is not fair. However, sooner or later everyone experiences an unexpected gift of grace.

Hurt has positive side effects, though they are usually seen only in retrospect. Prolonged struggles with difficulties can produce a sensitivity to pain in other people that enables its victims to become invaluable helpers. This is not to glorify pain, but only to state a fact.

Honesty Is the Best Policy

Truth fails to substantiate pervasive pessimism or rigid optimism. Good and bad exist side by side in most people's lives. Not uncommonly, the two appear intertwined. Jesus' pastoral metaphor of wheat and weeds growing together (Matt. 13:24–30) fits perfectly.

Live long enough, and you will know (if you don't know already) both joy and sorrow, pleasure and pain. You will have valid reasons to hurt and to hope. Experience defies the development of a single exclusive perspective on life—positive or negative. Often promise as well as pain results from an onslaught of problems.

Certain possibilities are predictable. Great joy accompanies the giving of yourself to another in love. But great vulnerability inheres in authentic love. A lover possesses no guarantees against hurt. Rejection or betrayal can ensue. If this happens, an avalanche of pain descends on you. However, cynicism is not inevitable. You only know the unfathomable ecstasy of love when you risk an experience that can produce horrendous hurt. So goes the nature of life. Be honest about it.

Tears fill some days just as laughter does others. Your capacity to frolic with elation makes you susceptible to bowing under grinding sorrow. Adventuresome actions often produce successes. But sometimes they end in failure.

Be negative if the situation calls for it. Calamities evoke severe negative emotions. Death, poverty, and violence rightly precipitate grief, anger, and anxiety. But life consists of more than troubles. Births occur. People reconcile their differences. Nations sign peace treaties. Reasons for gratitude and joy exist. A positive attitude can (and should) abound.

Be honest about what you experience. And react honestly to your experiences. No one set of circumstances forms a basis from which to judge all of life.

Recently I watched a TV sportscaster interview an outstanding major-league baseball pitcher. Critics were hounding this young man because of losses in his last two games. When the announcer asked if the criticism bothered him, the all-star player responded with great wisdom. "Not much. I know I'm never as bad as people think I am when I lose and never as good as people think I am when I win." What a great way to look at life! This young pitcher showed commendable honesty.

Cynicism severely hampers responsible coping in a difficult situation. Where hurt persists, cynicism hinders healing.

Cynics habitually denigrate the very values, attitudes, principles, and actions from which they can benefit. They castigate the means and opportunities that point to better health. Thus, cynics shoot themselves in the foot—or in the soul. Don't allow yourself to be counted among them.

Fight cynicism.

CHAPTER FIVE

Keep a Sense of Humor

Humor contributes inestimably to a person's ability to cope with the trauma produced when life tumbles in. Popular writer Gail Sheehy identifies humor as one of four coping devices found among people who have successfully overcome crises. Similarly, George Vaillant's research at the Harvard Medical School isolates humor as one of five major coping mechanisms employed by professional men under stress.[1] After conducting extensive studies on humor as an integral component in effective coping, Vera Robinson writes, "Certainly, there has been much support for the emotionally therapeutic value of humor as an adaptive coping behavior, as a catharsis for and relief of tension, as a defense against depression, as a sign of emotional maturity, and as a survival mechanism."[2]

Good humor does more than improve or enhance your attitude. Recent scientific data demonstrate that the best treatment for many physical problems combines proper medication with positive emotions. Humor nurtures both physiological and psychological health in people besieged by difficulties.

In many ways, humor functions like faith in helping us deal with the incompatibilities of life. When we are troubled and perplexed, humor enables us to manage disparities better and establish distinctions between the relative and the absolute. In fact, humor can build faith. As Donald Demaray asserts, "Humor sends pleasure coursing through our thought processes, assists in reestablishing perspective, opens our minds to new vistas of reality, and releases us from tension. Spiritually, it restores faith."[3]

Personally, I know I am in real trouble when I can no longer laugh. I despise the condition. Conversely, I realize I am getting better when I can experience hearty laughter once again. To enjoy a good sense of humor, then to lose it, and finally to recover the joy that accompanies robust laughter—laughter that shakes the body and frees the spirit—establishes the value of humor as nothing else.

Give Yourself Permission to Play

Play? You protest. That's ridiculous counsel. Life is falling in around me and you want me to take time to play? Things are far too serious right now for me to have any fun. What would my friends think if I started trying to be happy during this time when I should be grieving?

Often a crisis sets in motion a cycle of reactions that is difficult to halt but destructive if not stopped. Bad experiences pile up. Severity shrouds your life. A mixture of anger, grief, and regret assaults your outlook on life and produces worsening negative emotions. You need the relief provided by a good laugh, the health-giving presence of humor. But you reject all opportunities to encounter joy.

At first glance, the rationale that supports this cycle seems sound. "This is no time for fun. Let me get through all this heaviness and then I will be ready to experience some happiness." But a closer look reveals flawed thought. "Play is not a mood"[4] but, rather, an activity that takes place amid many moods. Not only can you play during a crisis—angered at circumstances, burdened with anxieties, and overwhelmed by responsibilities—you *should* play at this time. Play does not put off dealing with difficulties. Play is an important way of coping with them.

You will not be able to handle emotional heaviness successfully without periods of happiness. When you put off times

KEEP A SENSE OF HUMOR 59

of play until you get better, you deny yourself an essential ingredient in what you need to get better. Improved emotional health involves lighthearted play.

You need experiences of fun and laughter more than ever when you are at your worst. Meaning in life must not be reduced to a relentless execution of responsibility. In fact, commitment to an incessant acceptance of infinite responsibility destroys an individual. Everyone needs relief from the pressures of doing, having, and achieving—the kind of relief that comes in joyful play.

In times of crisis, however, seldom do humorous occasions filled with joking and the laughter of good humor take place serendipitously. To know a measure of joy amid hurt, you have to reach out for it, even plan for it.

During a period of critical financial depression, my wife and I rented a place near the beach and went there to play for several days. We could not afford it. Some of our friends questioned the wisdom of our action.

Bills had stacked up. For weeks, serious economic deficits in the family budget had tightened our emotional muscles, packed our chests with smothering stress, and quickened the pace of an already rapidly ticking relational time bomb. A physical, emotional, or relational crisis would only worsen our ability to cope with mounting financial problems. So we set aside a few dollars that could have only minimally reduced the balance due in one area of indebtedness and spent that money for a stretch of time to enjoy the seashore. We watched sunrises, chased crabs across the sand, ran in the rolling surf, mocked the cries of soaring sea gulls, and laughed heartily.

No miracles occurred while we were away. At least, no economic miracles. My wife and I returned home to face some wrenching decisions about finances. However, a time of play had relaxed our bodies, fed our spirits, clarified our values, and enhanced our ability to cope with our impending crisis. In retrospect, though we could not afford this fun experience in terms of dollars and cents, we could not have afforded to miss it in terms of emotional sense.

You know better than anyone else what brings lightness to your heart and a smile to your face. Perhaps it is a funny movie, a book of jokes, or a sitcom on television. Maybe you need to go on a fishing expedition or share a picnic lunch with a particularly good-natured friend. Whatever your best potential source of enjoyment may be, go for it.

Experts on human behavior have discovered that play often yields insights into deep-seated personal problems and points the way to possible solutions like no other activity. Without play, you sense life closing in around you, smothering you. In that situation, you cannot see anything beyond the immediate moment. And pain, panic, and desperation usually dominate that moment. Play contributes to a clear, objective, and comprehensive perspective on life—even (maybe particularly) on a troubled life. Periods of play provide creative promise-giving experiences.

Take seriously your need for pleasure. This counsel, applicable to life generally, takes on added importance in times of crisis.

Laugh!

That's right, laugh. Time-worn clichés labeling laughter as "good medicine" have a sound basis in fact. Laughter *is* good medicine, a superior coping mechanism.

In a pioneering book on the relationship between health, illness, healing, and emotion, Norman Cousins detailed the discoveries he made about the pain-relieving, health-inducing effects of laughter during his bout with a life-threatening illness.[5] One evening at Johns Hopkins University, I listened to Cousins discuss his twelve years of research exploring the power of laughter as a healing emotion and identifying laughter

KEEP A SENSE OF HUMOR

as a crucial factor in effective coping regardless of the nature of the problem. In the course of his research, Cousins collected overwhelming evidence, important for both patients and doctors, affirming the importance of laughter in the lives of people seeking to cope with various kinds of disaster.

How is this possible?

Emotionally, laughter releases crippling tension, counteracts debilitating sorrow, and facilitates improved discernment. Laughter alters moods, improves a person's self-image, transforms negativism into positivism, and reduces stress and depression.

When we can laugh at a situation we achieve a certain amount of transcendence in relation to that situation. Dramatic support for this truth comes from the noted psychologist Victor Frankl. Reflecting on a hellish period spent as a wartime captive in a Nazi compound, Frankl identifies laughter as *the* source of a perspective and hope that saved his life.[6]

To an extent, laughter reduces the control a crisis exercises over us and allows us to exert some control over the crisis. But laughter's power to enhance responsible coping goes beyond the emotions. The American Medical Association reports that every organ in the body responds positively to laughter.

Numerous studies have discovered that the brain is the source of multiple health-enhancing secretions. Good humor, specifically laughter, serves as a catalyst. Laughter translates into a biochemical reality wherein the brain produces natural painkillers called endorphins.

The kind of heightened emotion caused by laughter also results in a sizable increase in the number of red blood cells in a person's body. This development, in turn, strengthens an individual's immune system by producing cytotoxic T cells that attack and destroy diseased cells.

Laughter holds incredible power for a person seeking to cope with a crisis. Little wonder that many of the nation's major medical centers now show comic films to their most seriously ill patients. Other hospitals also include humorous materials among their therapeutic resources.

One expert in gelotology—the study of laughter—advises that a person should laugh at least fifteen times every day. According to this authority, three of these episodes should qualify as "belly laughs."[7]

"Great," you say. "That sounds good. But how do you do it? With my world crumbling around me, how can I possibly laugh?" Answering that question requires probing the depths of your convictions about life. For someone like the apostle Paul, faith provided a confidence that allowed him to laugh even at the threat of death. Truthfully, though, not everyone finds such sufficiency in that which exists inside them. For many folks, experiencing laughter during a crisis means asking for help.

Join a Joking Fellowship

Most crises contain barriers to laughter—embarrassment, rejection, risk, anxiety, criticism. The troubled person who manages to negotiate these difficulties successfully often fears that laughter, or displays of a good sense of humor, will seem foolish in the eyes of other people. Hit the fear of laughter head on and reach out to individuals who will not only help you laugh but join in your laughter.

In Africa, some primitive tribes designate a member of the community to restrain, entertain, and distract those persons in the fellowship who are bereaved. The individual who fills this role bears the title "joking partner."[8] How wise!

Beaten down by problems around us, we often need an uplift from friends. We act with great wisdom when we seek out a "joking partner" or find company in a joking fellowship. A significant dimension of crisis-related coping involves saying to a friend (or to friends), "Make me laugh," or, more subtly, scheduling time with people sure to cause laughter.

While doing research on clowns, I made an interesting discovery. In an autobiographical volume, Emmett Kelly, a longtime circus clown, observed that humorous entertainers seldom become suicidal. Though itinerant minstrels encounter a great deal of unhappiness and even tragedy, they retain the gift of laughter. As they make other people laugh, they learn to laugh at themselves. According to Kelly, in such laughter clowns find "a sort of spiritual second wind."[9] Of course, clowns have no monopoly on laughter. You too can claim the promise of Kelly's insight.

A fellowship of laughter can encourage anyone struggling with a crisis. If you are not a part of such a fellowship already, seek one out. You will be the better for it. And you will enjoy it.

Conceptions of humorous people as less than serious represent a fundamental misunderstanding of humor, concern, and personhood. Tragedy and comedy, tears and laughter, share a common source in the human psyche. Usually, a person unable to appreciate happiness during a crisis also lacks the capacity to understand real tragedy. Among individuals who have successfully coped with great difficulties, pleasure and pathos, like play and problems, complement rather than contradict each other.

Work on your sense of humor even as you seek to cope with your crisis. Neither labor denies the importance of the other or distracts from its effectiveness. The two—maintaining a good sense of humor and coping with a crisis—go together.

Two observations serve simultaneously as words of warning and words of encouragement regarding humor.

First, laugh when *you* want (or need) to laugh. Not all people possess the same sense of humor. Thus, what you see as hilarious, others may view differently. Do not allow that fact to concern you. You cannot afford to exhibit pleasure only when you sense that others will understand your laughter and share in it. Spontaneous laughter provides a freedom unattainable by way of judicious decisions or majority opinions on what qualifies as funny. Besides, humor does not have to make sense.

Second, your ability to laugh amid a crisis (and at a crisis) will threaten some people. Many individuals do not give themselves permission to joke about serious matters. Again, do not be deterred by that fact.

One evening several months after I had been hospitalized for depression, my wife and I were bantering with each other in the presence of several friends and a few acquaintances. After I made a particularly foolish wise crack, my wife said, "You better be careful. We will put you right back in the hospital." We both laughed, as did most of our friends. Several of the others present, however, hesitated even to smile. They squirmed uncomfortably. That was all right.

No reason exists to replace a health-giving dimension of your life with a sickness-inducing caution found in others. Keep in mind that a crisis is a time to be humorous as well as a time to be serious. Remember, too, H. G. Wells's astute observation that the crisis of today will be the joke of tomorrow.

Keep a sense of humor.

CHAPTER SIX

Pray

Before you react to this counsel, do not associate my suggestion to pray with escaping into the language of piety. At the same time, do not imagine that following this advice means repeating familiar phrases drawn from religious rituals, speaking aloud words that seem appropriate in addressing God, or parroting impressive, spiritual-sounding petitions picked up from other people.

Pray. Speak to God in your own words and in your own manner. Authentic prayer requires you to open yourself completely to God and with total honesty place before God your concerns, questions, doubts, and declarations.

Aghast at the destruction wrought by the Spanish Civil War on the island of Majorca, the French novelist George Bernanos observed, "Our rages, daughters of despair, creep and squirm like worms. Prayer is the only form of revolt which remains upright."[1] All who hurt understand.

Prayer holds nothing back in communication with God. Everything can and should be said. Everything! God invites us to tell it like it is, to be totally honest about what we have done, how we feel, and the way in which we see ourselves. Offering anything else to God fails to qualify as real prayer.

Praying is an essential activity in coping with a life-shattering crisis. Psychiatrist William Sadler writes, "When we set ourselves to the work of collecting or re-collecting the scattered pieces of ourselves, we begin a task which, if carried to its natural conclusions, ultimately becomes prayer."[2]

Don't Worry About Mechanics

Unfortunately, people often get distracted from praying by a quest for the proper way (or the "best" way) to pray. Seeking answers to mechanics-oriented questions replaces speaking to God naturally. Cries of the heart give way to inquiries from the mind. Should I sit, kneel, stand, or lie prone? When is the best time? Do I have to close my eyes? Should I address God as "Thou," "Thee," or "You"?

Forget all such concerns about logistics. When you pray, you speak to One who loves you with an unconditional love, accepts you for who you are, and seeks to embrace you with incomprehensible grace. Protocol and propriety do not enter the picture. Formality is a non sequitur. Only honesty and trust matter.

The place and time of prayer have virtually no significance. You can pray anywhere and any time. No walls or doors have yet been built that can shut out the presence of God. Occasionally you may want to seek out a secret place in which to pray alone. But that does not preclude praying while leaning on your desk, pacing a sales floor, standing beside an empty grave, or sitting behind the steering wheel of your car waiting for a traffic light to change. Most of the geographical sites where praying takes place are totally nonreligious in appearance. Look at Job, the Old Testament sufferer, pouring out his heart to God while perched atop a heap of ashes.

Posture merits little concern in relation to prayer. Some folks fold their hands in front of their faces as a gesture of reverence before God when praying. Your prayer may as easily consist of screaming to God about your pain while pounding your hands on a tabletop. Kneeling to pray can indicate worship and submission. Or it can be no more than a gesture that shifts attention from the substance to the show of prayer. A bowed head fails as a substitute for a devoted heart. Posture in prayer really matters very little.

A preoccupation with the general pattern of prayer can compromise the content of a specific prayer. Prayer counselors properly admonish people to engage in adoration, praise, confession, repentance, intercession, dedication, and thanksgiving. These suggestions help. Each of these expressions of prayer proves exceedingly worthwhile. However, you should not allow such a broad understanding of prayer to prevent you from approaching God with a specific need.

Your prayer to God is a conversation with One who loves you supremely. The mood in which you speak doesn't matter. George Buttrick, a careful student as well as a model practitioner of prayer, helpfully observed that "there are no forms of prayer, any more than there are brick walls across the stream of conversation or fences in the sky."[3] Eventually you will get around to most of the moods of prayer and at various times speak to God adoringly, penitently, and thankfully. Seldom, though, will any one of your prayers encompass all of the possible moods of prayer. That's fine. Don't worry about it. Talk to God with stark honesty.

In a particularly troublesome moment, you may not feel like praise as you rush to a confession: "God, I have got to have your help." That's all right, forge ahead. Similarly, intercession can stand alone. You do not have to appease God by specifying reasons for thanksgiving before requesting God to provide strength for a problem-ridden friend. Praying in panic, you may rush right past any words of formal address to God as a prelude to what you want to say and blurt out, "My wife is in big trouble. God, please give her peace, security, and a sense of direction." God hears with understanding.

Praying means pouring out your heart and opening up your life to God. No one else can dictate how you do that. Be yourself. Pray in your own way.

Be Honest

Prayer does not exist without honesty. No accumulation of religious terminology can take the place of personal truth-telling. Basically, no rules govern prayer. However, honesty in prayer is mandatory.

This one requirement for prayer may threaten you, at least at first. For social approval or self-protection, to avoid embarrassing questions, or for other reasons, you may have mastered the art of deception. You can look well though hurting badly, feign confidence when in a panic, and declare aloud, "I'm just fine," when you have never been worse. Faking can become a way of life. You probably despise it. But you fear testing the alternative.

Honesty in prayer is different. Honest prayers liberate rather than burden, comfort rather than produce anxiety. Of course, vulnerability accompanies honesty before God even as it accompanies truthfulness with your peers. In relation to God, though, you become open to love, grace, and redemption, not to the barbs of second-guessing critics and the attacks of self-appointed judges. Truth in prayer is a blessing, not a curse; a way to healing, not an invitation to more hurt.

For me, experiences of prayer often provide the only moments of relief and sanity to be enjoyed in the course of a hectic day. Professional duties require an air of confidence that reassures clients and implies a promise of help. A realistic distrust of competitors sustains a carefully choreographed public relations routine intended to hide weaknesses, fears of failure, weariness with work, and guilt over wrongdoing. However, approaching God in prayer dramatically differs from all that. Masks come off. Subterfuge is set aside. Feelings are laid bare. Words flow unmeasured. Honesty fills the soul with refreshment akin to that provided by a cooling breeze on an unbearably hot day. With prayer come cleansing, unburdening, understanding, and peace.

You can say to God what you cannot (or will not) say to anyone else: I'm scared to death! I am sick of my job. My desires are out of control. I want to run away, far away, from everything and everybody. I am beginning to hate my husband. This grief has got to end. I am such a failure. I despise successful people. I am ready to give up.

Not only can you speak to God with devastating honesty, you can do so without fear of rejection. God will not desert you because of what you say, think, or feel. Or because of who you are.

"But what if I am angry at God and ready to chuck what few beliefs I still hold?" you ask. That's all right too. God prefers honesty to deception regardless of content. God can respond much better to attacks, questions, and disagreements than to attempts at camouflage that insult God's wisdom and empty platitudes couched in a perception of a God without grace. God prefers to be taken seriously, even if by denial, rather than ignored or approached with superficiality and dishonesty.

Be Persistent

Prayers can be planned studiously as well as formed spontaneously. Though prayer can be a welcome experience of relief and renewal, sometimes prayer involves hard work. Over the long haul, discipline in prayer is as important as devotion. Amid a crisis, one prayer will not suffice. Pray with persistence. Pray often.

At a crucial point in his life, Howard Thurman made a resolution regarding persistence in prayer. Later he wrote of the discipline involved. "I am conditioning my nervous system so that after tonight, until the end of the journey, it will be impossible for me inadvertently to step out of bed onto the floor without first making a circle of light to guide me"[4] What a terrific model.

When you are caught up in the chaos of a crisis, prayer may seem like a luxury you cannot afford or a responsibility that will have to wait for a better moment to receive your attention. When your troubles even remotely relate to religion, prayer can appear as an obstacle you prefer to avoid.

You do not have to feel like praying in order to pray. C. S. Lewis concluded that he had to say his prayers whether or not he felt devout, just as he had to study grammar if he were ever to read the poets. Your need to pray and the value of your prayers do not depend on your wants and wishes. A period of your life without prayer constitutes the spiritual counterpart to a serious asthmatic condition—breathing becomes difficult, the world shrivels, life is threatened. Whether or not you feel like praying, you must pray if you are to cope and survive. Persist in your prayers.

In some situations, our sense of God's absence makes prayer very difficult. Only yesterday a troubled person spoke to me out of deep hurt. "Where is God in all of this?" she asked with a twinge of bitterness. Such an attitude must not be used as an argument against praying. To the contrary, confessions of a sense of godforsakenness or aloneness contribute to the substance of meaningful prayers. John Berryman once prayed, "We know you're there, Lord, the sweat is—we're here."[5] Complaints about God's absence need not be denied or silenced.

Harry Emerson Fosdick used to tell people that refraining from prayer because God did not seem near made no sense. He explained that God will seem nearer only to the person who prays.[6]

But what if I can't say anything? What if words do not come? you ask. Don't worry about it. Word counts and eloquence do not impress God. Brevity characterizes many of life's most profound prayers: "Help!" "O God," "Deliver me," "Forgive me," "Guide me," "Save me." Other communiqués to God defy any articulation at all. Occasionally we can reach for the heavens only by means of our sighs and groans.

Imagine a Conversation with God

Only fools play God. Danger marks such mockery. However, trying to imagine a dialogue with God—conceptualizing God's words, spirit, and will as well as yours—can be beneficial. Especially when you are having trouble with prayer, give it a try.

Assume the role of God. Think what you, as God, would say to a person like yourself who attempts to communicate. Be guided by a few givens drawn from certainties about God: God loves you with an unfathomable love. God wants to hear exactly what you think, feel, and say—all of it. God responds to every part of your prayer with an invitation and encouragement for you to continue praying. You cannot say anything to God in your prayer that will cause God to stop listening to you, responding to you, or caring for you.

With those truths about God in mind, activate your imagination. Engage God in a conversation. Try to project God's responses to your prayerful petitions. Your dialogue with God could go something like this:

God, I want to pray. I really need to pray. But I'm uncomfortable. I don't know exactly what to think, say, or do.

I want to hear anything you want to say, all that you need to say. Maybe talking about the positives in your life can get you started. For what are you thankful?

Even that is tough. Right now I have a hard time seeing any positives in my life. Being thankful in the middle of grief and serious trouble is almost beyond my abilities. But I'll give it a try. I'm thankful for the possibilities of prayer and for this opportunity to pray. I'm glad you gave us the Bible. I'm grateful for Jesus. I'm thankful for the many blessings you bestow on us.

Wait. That doesn't sound like you. You're saying what you think I want to hear. Drop the formality and speak your mind. What's troubling you? Tell me about your needs.

I'm worried. Really worried. My emotional stability is as fragile as my financial security.

I'm tired. I am weary of trying to keep up a good front. I'm tired of seeking to be strong for the sake of everybody else. I want to crash. I want to feel free to be who I am—a weak, frightened, hurting person. I need rest.

And I'm mad! I am . . . Let's just leave it at that.

No. Please define the targets of your anger. It can help.

I am mad at people whom I trusted and shouldn't have. I am fed up with friends who raise false hopes by making promises they never intend to keep. I feel as if I could physically attack those individuals who, dripping with syrupy sweetness, say "I understand" when they don't have the foggiest idea about the pain I am experiencing.

Maybe I shouldn't say it, but I am also mad at you, God. It seems to me you could do something about all the hurt in life if you really wanted to.

I have got to have help in getting rid of this anger. It's killing me. I am having as much trouble living with myself as with other people.

Tell me about yourself specifically.

I have screwed up my life. That's the only thing I have done a good job at. I made a series of bad decisions at work, immoral decisions. I got involved in a business deal that was as stupid as it was wrong. My integrity unraveled like a ball of twine rolling down a steep hill. It didn't just happen; I pushed it.

Wanting something for nothing, I gamble. Desiring to get back at people who have hurt me, I act vindictively. Hoping for even a fleeting moment of good feelings, I search for happiness in all the wrong places.

I have hurt other people. I betrayed a friendship. My family can no longer understand me—or, worse, trust me.

My beliefs have faded as my sins have mounted.

I forgive you. And I will help you if that is your desire.

But I haven't asked yet. I did not say, "God be merciful to me a sinner" or "All we like sheep have gone astray." I thought I had to use those words.

You are forgiven. How can I help you right now?

Oh, God, that's the greatest gift, forgiveness. I can make it with that. But there's more. Help me find some time to rest and enough peace inside to take advantage of that time.

Increase my capacity for love and enable me to better demonstrate my love for my family.

Help me be more understanding.
Strengthen my faith.

Don't hesitate to prod me, God, if I go too long without praying. This is not easy for me. I will probably try to find any excuse I can to keep from praying. But I want to pray more.

Your honesty delights me. Praying is often not easy. But it doesn't have to be. Count on my help. And my continued love.

Amen to that. Amen.

Amid a crisis, moments arrive when you feel you have done all you can do—and indeed you may have. You are ready to give up. Trust becomes crucial at this point. Trust allows you to give up by placing your situation in the hands of God: not as a cop-out, not as an act of weakness or despair, but as an act of faith.

Praying is like floating on water.[7] We float only when we quit fighting the water, give up, relax, and trust the water to hold us. God desires to hold us. And God doesn't even mind the fighting.

The only non-negotiable is honesty.

Pray.

CHAPTER SEVEN

Channel Your Anger

Note carefully the specific nature of this counsel: Channel your anger. Don't deny it. Refrain as well from attempts to repress it.

Anger is a fact of life. Crisis situations almost invariably involve anger. Responsible coping with a troublesome problem necessitates successfully dealing with anger—the anger involved and the anger it generates.

Reason helps. Intellectual prowess holds great promise for finding satisfactory solutions to critical problems. Analytical abilities and a capacity to strategize alternative responses serve a person well in the face of difficulties. However, regardless of the nature of a situation, you will never get to the positive contributions made by rational processes without an honest confrontation with your angry emotions.

Left alone, anger acts like a dangerous tropical depression. Mounting frustrations, disappointments, and anxieties swell normal emotional breezes into psychic blasts that threaten to devastate a person's perspective. In time, warm currents of anger intensify both in strength and heat as they swirl around inside an individual. Churning resentment combines with irrational fury. Soon, a full-blown storm with hurricane-force winds thrashes the person's well-being and lashes out at everyone and everything in the person's path. When such fully developed anger sweeps across the landscape of an individual's life, the wreckage is usually so pervasive that good intentions, noble goals, and helpful relationships lie in ruins right alongside all that is bad.

A minor incident makes a major point. While taking a

shortcut home at one in the morning, a motorist had a flat tire. Then he discovered that he could not change tires because the jack in his car trunk did not work. Looking down the unfamiliar road in dismay, the fellow spotted a darkened farmhouse not far away. He hated the thought of awakening the farmer, but he needed assistance. Maybe he owned a jack.

As the disgruntled motorist walked toward the farmhouse, his anger took control. An active imagination painted an imposing and further infuriating picture. The man surmised that he would upset the farmer, by awakening him at this hour, and anger him to the point that even if he owned a jack he would refuse to loan it. Rampant emotions ruled. When the farmer opened the door to his house in response to the beleaguered traveler's knocks, the motorist shouted in his face, "Keep your old jack!"[1]

Change the image. Anger is a fire. Handle it responsibly and you can benefit from it. Ignore it, or deal with it irresponsibly, and anger will destroy you (burn you up or burn you out). Other people may also be victimized by the blaze.

You cannot play with fire without getting hurt. Or with anger.

Own Up to Your Anger

Admit your anger. Claim it. I write this fully aware that giving this advice is much easier than implementing it.

Innumerable pressures seek to prevent up-front personal acknowledgments of anger. Our culture prizes (and praises) the unflappable person—always in control, never ruffled, perpetually cool, above rancor. A powerful though mistaken spirituality confuses piety and passivity as it commends both. Within families, parents frequently respond to their children's anger by labeling the emotion as a personal weakness or, worse still, as a work of the devil. Subsequently, many people deem denials of anger as more appropriate than acknowledgments of anger. Wrong!

Actually, anger represents health; it conveys a positive emotion. Sure, it can go bad. Anger can be abused or become abusive. However, this important emotion must not be denied because of its potential for evil. Negative consequences of anger can be avoided. Anger can be very helpful to people in trouble.

Anger means you care. Lewis Smedes dubs anger "the executive power of human decency."[2] Why be embarrassed about that? Anger requires no apologies. You will probably find anger most intense among the people with whom you are most intimate.

Repetitious denials of anger fuel a quiet rage almost certain to induce depression inwardly and foment destruction outwardly. Illness replaces health. Decision-making skills deteriorate. Behavior moves toward extremes. And people get hurt. No one suffers more, though, than the person trying to act as if the anger does not exist.

Focus Your Anger

Anger can fool you. You think you have everything under control and suddenly anger erupts, appearing at the wrong time and mystifying—sometimes attacking—innocent people. For example, a businesswoman's anger over a situation at work precipitates a vicious verbal attack on her daughter, when the girl simply requests an advance on her allowance.

Not long ago I spoke with a friend whose appearance screamed trouble. "What's wrong?" I asked. He responded immediately, "I'm really mad." "Who are you mad at?" I continued. After pausing to think, he said, "I don't know. I'm just fighting mad."

Red flags went up in my mind. Warning signs dotted that

conversation. Unfocused anger is like a loaded shotgun in the hands of a deranged sniper. When the firing starts, shot flies in all directions, causing widespread suffering and devastation.

Define the target of your anger. That sounds simple enough. It isn't. You may well need help to get your anger properly in focus. If so, ask for it.

Many situations illustrate the importance of focused anger. A woman repeatedly lashes out at her husband; their relationship deteriorates, and all attempts at correction fail. Actually, the woman harbors a deep-seated, terrible anger toward her mother, but she will not (or maybe cannot) acknowledge that reality, so she continually attacks her husband. Similarly, a young man spits out a series of sacriligious comments about the Christian faith. Faith is not the anger-inducing issue, though. Longtime acquaintances are the problem. Explosive anger toward people in his home church gnaws at this fellow's innards. Members of the congregation recently demonstrated in dramatic fashion (to his dismay, disappointment, and embarrassment) their complicity with racism. Unless both these individuals—the wife and the young man—get their anger in focus, identify its source, and work on the true causes of their problems, they will continue to hurt innocent people as well as worsen their own situations.

To claim the benefits of your anger, you must identify the center of its focus. Anger at your spouse can be resolved. Together the two of you can find ways to eradicate its causes. For that to happen, though, you have to know that your spouse is indeed the target. Otherwise, you will be working on the symptoms of your anger, not on its cause.

"What if I am angry at God?" Fearful of the repercussions of such an admission, bearers of this question usually ask it in a whisper. Without reason, actually. God prefers people's angry protests over being ignored or considered gullable enough to be pleased by the superficial silence of an artificial devotion. Anger at God means you take God seriously.

People develop anger toward God for understandable reasons. Telling comments trace their stories: "If God would, God could do something about my little girl's suffering." "God just lets evil win one battle after another, leaving moral people defeated."

God commends, not condemns, honesty. Anger toward God precedes a deeper understanding of God and the nature of God's involvement in life. Getting your anger at God in focus raises the possibility of significant spiritual growth.

Express Your Anger Appropriately

Though a person denies anger verbally and represses anger visibly, the anger will find an outlet—causing terrible headaches, forming a stomach ulcer, inflicting insomnia. Anger always finds release one way or another. You cannot stop it. Why not opt for appropriate expressions and damage control?

Anger continuously denied or repressed leads to emotional illness. Count on it. Both cynicism and depression result from sustained, undeclared—and thus unresolved—anger. You may be able to hide your anger from others and from yourself, but the negative conditions produced by hidden anger will be obvious to everyone.

Is it possible to express anger appropriately? Paul thought so. That conviction motivated his counsel, "Be angry but do not sin" (Eph. 4:26). I agree.

Obedience to that biblical admonition takes great effort. I know lots of people who tell me they are "mad as hell." That's easy. Anyone can experience diabolical rage. The real challenge is to move in the opposite direction—to become "mad as heaven." That takes work. However, during a crisis, such hard labor contributes mightily to effective coping.

Responsible anger involves discipline. A wise person exerts all the control necessary to squelch temper tantrums. These "fits of anger" (excellent terminology) help no one, least of all the angry individual. Uncontrolled anger wreaks havoc in a person's life and inevitably stirs up a hellish chaos.

Heavenly oriented anger expresses itself constructively rather than destructively. Trying to heed the biblical injunction about anger, we must exercise great care to assure that during a period of anger we do not damage long-standing relationships, tear down lines of communication between ourselves and institutions of help, and destroy our good name.

Look at the matter selfishly. Out-of-control anger hurts the enraged person more than anyone else. An individual with a passion for angry retaliation will suffer as a result of this driving motivation.

Anger vented irresponsibly in a crisis stirs up more trouble and makes a terrible mess. Bad circumstances worsen. Furiously flailing away at everybody and everything, taking cheap shots at opponents, and working to wreck institutions in disfavor may provide immediate emotional release. But the cost is high—a sacrifice of integrity, a compromise of compassion, and a dissipation of self-worth. Angry people bent on the destruction of others ultimately destroy themselves.

Capitalize on the Energy Generated by Your Anger

Hope resides in timely anger that inspires positive action. Both in Moses the patriarch and Jesus the Messiah anger existed as a positive, creative force for good. They are superior models. Anger at oppression incites the work of liberation. Anger at dishonesty strengthens demands for integrity. Anger caused by injustice activates a passion for justice.

Call up the figure of fire again. Like fire, anger generates incredible amounts of energy.

During the 1992 summer Olympic games in Barcelona,

Spain, a gymnastic coach expressed great pleasure at seeing signs of anger in one of his prize pupils. This young girl, favored to win a medal, made a costly error in her first performance. Her mistake and the low scores from the judges that it prompted filled her with fury. During an interview, the experienced coach explained that she would score significantly higher points in her next round of exercises because she was fueled by anger. Her anger would provide a strength which, when controlled by her carefully honed discipline, she could use to her advantage.

When harnessed and directed responsibly, energy produced by anger sustains efforts that enhance the quality of people's lives. The application of that principle reaches far beyond the realm of gymnastics. Abolitionists, civil rights leaders, environmentalists, war protesters, and political reformers feed on an anger caused by the evil conditions they attack. A carefully controlled rage sustains herculean efforts aimed at a better world. Remove the anger from these people's lives and much of their energy departs with it.

What happens socially also occurs personally. A mother reels in response to her son's death by suicide. Eventually anger emerges within her, a broadside of anger with the power to destroy her. Fortunately this woman seizes the energy spawned by her anger and uses it to launch a movement aimed at helping young people in trouble and parents who have lost troubled sons or daughters.[3]

Anger at the dangers precipitated by a bad habit generates the strength needed to break the habit. Anger over the ineptness of an organization spawns the energy to initiate major organizational reforms. Anger at dishonesty in interpersonal relationships breeds the will and empowers the way to challenge superficiality and develop commitments marked by maturity.

Properly channeled anger signals hope. Anger indicates you care. You will face into an anger-producing situation rather than ignore it or walk away from it. More precisely, anger means you care enough about a problem or a person to act to

CHANNEL YOUR ANGER

get rid of the conditions that spark your anger. Real promise resides in that disposition.

Your anger can fuel actions that eradicate the cause of your anger. Harness that power. Without it, you may not have the strength even to begin to take action on what must be done. With it, you may be able to cope with crisis in a manner that actually creates the promise of a better future.

When unacknowledged, unfocused, or mishandled, anger can worsen any situation considerably. Ignored, anger diminishes your coping skills even as it complicates the difficulties you face. Watch your anger conscientiously. Work on it and with it.

Anger does not—cannot—eliminate a crisis, solve a problem, or heal hurt. However, properly handled, anger sets in motion actions that can accomplish all these desired results. Remember, though, none of that happens accidentally. You must relate to your anger with intentionality, discipline, and sustained attention. When that is done, anger holds great promise for responsible coping.

Channel your anger.

CHAPTER EIGHT

Renew Your Dreams

Crises force us into situations we would never choose to enter if we had an alternative. Not surprisingly, negative reactions mount. Hopes disintegrate. Disillusionment develops. Grief and disappointment breed disorientation. Insecurity runs rampant. However, within this haystack of hurt, a needle of hope can be found.

In a situation shaped, if not created, by crisis, an opportunity to start over exists, a chance to begin again. Some folks refer to this as "a new lease on life," but that probably sounds too positive.

You did not desire this opportunity. It was forced upon you. By no means do you welcome the situation. As far as you can see, problems caused by it greatly outnumber any positives created by it. Nevertheless, minimal promise can be found among the multiple difficulties that haunt you. Discovering this promise and dreaming of new possibilities become vital components of the work of coping.

Certainly you would never decide to lose your job suddenly or opt to be left alone because of the tragic death of your spouse. Each of these occurrences imposes a high level of stress, engenders terrific grief (often intermingled with anger), and threatens emotional paralysis. However, with joblessness comes an opportunity to think about a new job, perhaps employment that sparks long-absent excitement. Most likely you would not have thought much about alternative jobs as long as you were gainfully employed. Almost certainly you would not have forfeited your paychecks to pursue other responsibilities, regardless of their attractiveness. But now this can be done. The opportunity remains unwanted (and maybe resented), but it is there. Amid the worries of unpaid bills, job applications to fill out, and insurance needs to address, a potential for creativity presents itself. You can think about what you would like to do next, what you really want to do with the rest of your life. It's almost like returning to the beginning of your professional career. Only this time you approach the starting line with considerably more insight and wisdom than you did the first time around.

Please do not misunderstand. Unemployment merits no glory. It is misery. Prolonged unemployment carries devastating consequences. But in that bad situation, you can find a window through which to look at life afresh and dream of what could develop.

Similar possibilities exist amid the grinding grief caused by the death of a spouse. In no way can any new potential compensate for the immeasurable worth of the person lost. But new opportunities present themselves along with terrible difficulties. As the initial shock of hurt subsides and thoughts begin to clear, previously unraised questions can be answered. "What can I do in this new situation that I could not do before? With no one for whom I have daily responsibility, how do I want to spend my time?"

As you seize the positive opportunities that exist in an altered life situation, avoid mind tricks and word games. You have no obligation to call a bad situation "good." The sole purpose of your coping involves an attempt to wring any "good" possible out of a predominantly bad situation. You can dream while sorting through relational, vocational, and emotional rubble as well as while sitting on a mountaintop calculating the extent of your successes.

Look Forward

Raise your head, open your eyes, and look forward. I know that is not easy. Crises can make these simple actions seem like monumental tasks.

Despair bows your head as it bends your back. Grief and anxiety cause you to close your eyes in an attempt to escape temporarily from pressing problems. Regrets and guilt leave you staring down at your feet or looking back over your shoulder. Do whatever you must to overcome these tendencies. If you give in to them, they will block your immediate vision of what surrounds you and prevent you from dreaming about what can lie ahead.

The past exerts a terrific pull. Serious troubles in the present intensify its magnetic force. Unless you resist this powerful attraction, memory may take you captive. Questions of "What if I had been there?" "What should I have done differently?" and "Why didn't I see what was happening?" dominate your thoughts. Sighs of "If only I had not acted so quickly," "Those were such good times," and "Life will never again be the same" zap your emotions. If this happens, you will not be able even to peer into the future, much less dream about it.

Memory can be very tricky. Selective reflections about earlier days rob you of a comprehensive, and thus realistic, view of the past. Extremes prevail. You recall only the good of earlier times, or only the bad. Consequently, you see the past either as much better or much worse than it actually was. Longing to go back to when life was "the best it will ever be" or dwelling on a past that was so terrible that life can never be very good, you do not care about coping with the present. And as far as you are concerned, the future will have to take care of itself. Dreams succumb to death by abortion. New visions will never be conceived.

Look forward. Learn from the past, but do not live in the past. Recognize the troubles of the present, but do not set up residence among them. A trite old piece of poetic verse describes two men locked behind bars. One stares down at the mud beneath the window in his cell. The other looks through a window at the stars. What a powerful image!

You can only see the new and exciting possibilities that fill the future if you open your eyes, look forward, and scan the horizon. Look. A sharp vision of what can be starts the adrenaline coursing through your body, sends your spirit soaring, and makes planning for the future an integral part of coping with the present.

Frankly, you may not be able to look ahead alone. If not, seek help. Turn to a trusted friend or consult someone who has gone through a crisis similar to yours. Be honest about your situation and request assistance. "I'm bogged down. I can't see anything but negatives. I can barely lift my head. Would you please help me see if any positive potential exists in my life? I would appreciate your giving me specific suggestions about modes of thought that could prompt a helpful, commanding vision." If you don't know anyone with whom you can engage in such a conversation informally, you would do well to secure the services of a skilled professional.

For many people struggling with problems, religious faith provides the muscles needed to look forward. Confronted by numerous opponents, hounded by messengers of discouragement, and battling a body-bending despondency, a writer of an ancient psalm cried to God, "But you, O LORD, are . . . the one who lifts up my head" (Ps. 3:3). What a striking image. What a wonderful truth!

Do not miss whatever good potential resides in the present moment or any attractive promise that the future may hold by failing to raise your head and see it. Even if you do not feel capable of acting immediately on what you see, the vision itself will do you inestimable good.

Establish Your Priorities

Learn from people facing a terminal illness and from individuals who have survived a close scrape with death. Such folks usually display a determination to live every day of their lives as if it were their last. Not uncommonly they reorder and radicalize their priorities—elevating matters of the heart, cherishing relationships, valuing experiences of genuine joy, giving themselves only to tasks they view as important, prizing risk, caring little about what other people think of their decisions and actions, and focusing on an abundant life.

The crisis you face can prompt a similar reordering of priorities. No guarantees exist, though. Discipline and initiative help bring about such a development. With effort, a bad situation can be the context in which you do the kind of priority-oriented decision-making that paves the way to a fulfilling life.

Actually, some crises represent the worst consequences of a long history of misplaced priorities. A woman finally achieves the professional recognition she has sought for years, only to realize she has no one with whom to celebrate the accomplishment because she has sacrificed durable relationships on the altar of success. As their last child leaves home following their thirtieth wedding anniversary, a couple begins to come apart because both partners have invested themselves in the children so exclusively that neither has nurtured a meaningful relationship with the other. A recognition of misordered values in the past, as painful as that is, can form the foundation on which you construct a new order of priorities to serve as the framework around which to build a promising future.

Not all crises submit to such easy analysis, though. Many periods of trouble cannot be explained by previously misplaced values. Problems often seem to be inexplicable, irrational, unjust broadsides against everything fair and valuable. Even then, however, dreams of new priorities can be poured into the crucible of pain.

Frequently, crises become occasions for dramatic reversals in people's priorities. While in the hospital recovering from a heart attack, a man who has been preoccupied with professional accomplishments for profit decides to concentrate on volunteer acts of personal service. As she begins a second marriage, a highly organized, rigidly scheduled woman throws away her appointment book, eager to experience the happiness of flexibility and the excitement of spontaneity.

When you are faced by a future more open than desired and challenged to chart an unsought course, reflect carefully on where, throughout your life, you have found the greatest joy, fulfillment, and peace as well as on what has filled you with the most frustration, disappointment, and despair. Then establish priorities that maximize your possibilities for enjoying life.

Evaluate Your Resources

Renewing dreams differs significantly from repetitious flights of fantasy. Taking an inventory of personal resources properly accompanies defining your vision. Without a consideration of whether or not you can do what you want to do, you set yourself up for disappointment, frustration, and maybe outright failure. Then your problems worsen rather than recede.

Dreamers appreciate (rather than resent or oppose) research and consultation related to the implementation of their visions. They answer important questions, either alone or with assistance: Do I need to borrow any money? Would I be better off with a partner? Should I enroll for more education? Conceptualizing a new future often requires conversations with a financial analyst, taking a battery of aptitude tests, and speaking with various experts about the specific demands inherent in various directions of involvement.

Without a vision people perish, yes. But people *with* a vision can also perish, especially if that vision has no basis in or relationship to reality. Dreamers cannot avoid counting the cost of their dreams without courting major problems. In no way should this observation discourage dreaming or pour cold water on creative thinking. Its sole purpose is to encourage actions that enhance the likelihood of seeing creative visions fulfilled. As one encourager of visions observes, "Our creativity grows with the ability to hold the possible and the actual . . . in tension."[1]

Develop Strategies

While you dream, answer the question, "How do I get there from here?" That exercise greatly contributes to envisioning the future helpfully.

Excited by new priorities and confident about available resources, good dreamers establish strategies by which their hopes can be realized. Chart your personal course of action. Do as much strategizing as you can on your own. However, do not hesitate to benefit from the insights of people who have already traveled roads similar to the one you intend to take.

Any worthwhile strategy includes a time to begin. Unduly delaying that moment can rob you of the enthusiasm inspired by the promise of realizing your vision.

Even if you cannot see the last step on your envisioned journey, you must at least be able to see the first step. Otherwise, devoid of a strategy, you will be paralyzed by your dream rather than motivated. Your vision will become a burden adding to your problems rather than a source of liberation from them.

You may have to practice great patience before seeing your dream realized. But impatience can also be virtuous. Moments arrive when a dream needs to be tested. The next step is clear, and it is time to take it. Additional thought must give way to action. At that point, a failure to act can strike a death blow to your dream. Test the dream. Act.

A favorite story of former President John F. Kennedy makes the point. A French marshal told his gardener to plant a seedling in his garden plot. The gardener protested, "But the seed won't flower for one hundred years." "Then by all means," the marshal said, "plant it right now." Such a spirit of urgency properly pervades a good dream and creates in the dreamer a driving desire to get on with life.

Periods of trouble force us to evaluate, revise, and renew our dreams. Or perhaps they cause us to begin to dream again.

RENEW YOUR DREAMS

We do not like the situations in which we find ourselves. But we do appreciate any positive potential we can find within them.

Long-term dreams fill us with helpful anticipation and keep us going. Short-term dreams promise more immediate satisfaction and sustain our commitment to those visions that will only be fulfilled in the future. Most important of all, though, is the fact that as long as we are dreaming we show confidence that we have a future.

Renew your dreams.

CHAPTER NINE

Exercise Faith

"What does faith have to do with it? Faith did not keep me from getting into this mess. How can it help me out?" Many persons seeking to cope with severe situations voice such protests.

To exercise faith, you need to know the nature of faith. Do not confuse faith with magic. Do not imagine faith to be a form of immunization against problems, or an escape from them. Living by faith differs dramatically from bartering with God—offering platitudinous praises in exchange for receiving divine protection from all difficulties.

Real faith holds no illusions and makes no claims about a trouble-free life. To the contrary, many people first discover the meaning of authentic faith while trying to cope with severe adversities. The most exemplary models of faith do not close their eyes to harsh facts. To exercise faith means to face all of life—successes and failures, comforts and difficulties—with faith.

Faith forms a strong foundation. It provides a stabilizing support for people whose world seems rocked by a prolonged earthquake measuring ten on the Richter scale. Faith's strength stems from its substance. As God inspires faith, God instills faith. God's actions in the past, presence in the present, and promises for the future constitute "the assurance of things hoped for, the conviction of things not seen" (Heb. 11:1).

Fantasy and faith have nothing in common. Pretense, make-believe, and denial regarding the dangers, difficulties, and demands presented by crises do not qualify as faith. Faith trades in reality and history.

A much-quoted cliché about faith dangerously misrepresents

the truth. Faith is not a blind leap into the dark. A confident, eyes-wide-open embrace of the presence and promises of God in all situations best characterizes faith. Assurances of what can be expected from God derive from reflections on God's actions in the past. The God of the exodus and resurrection never fails to act redemptively on behalf of people in trouble, to extend the possibility of deliverance to individuals seeking freedom from captivity, and to offer to lift the loads of people bent from carrying heavy burdens. If faith involves a leap, faith leaps into light.

Still, faith does not always come easily. Many barriers to belief hinder spiritual development. Not uncommonly, the most sizable roadblocks to faith are found in human personalities. A troubled individual desperately turns to a church for assistance, only to discover a response that hurts more than it helps. A sense of disappointment develops, sometimes even a feeling of outright betrayal, as individuals who boisterously acclaim their loyalty to the gospel turn their backs on friends in need and reflect the litigious nature of culture rather than the generous grace of God.

"Faith doesn't work!" an embittered woman asserts. "The gospel can't survive in this world. I trust God but not people, not even those who identify themselves as 'the people of God.'" Not only have I heard that declaration more than once, I have used some of the same words myself.

Failures among people, however, do not justify debunking the value of faith in God. Faith's value cannot be accurately judged by the actions of individuals who abuse faith even while claiming it. The value, power, and character of faith reside in the nature of God, who makes faith possible and offers it to everyone as a gift.

Recognize God as Revealed in Jesus Christ

To a remarkable extent, your concept of God determines the content of your faith. Too much is at stake to embrace erroneous impressions. Personal experiences and communal perceptions properly inform your view of God. Much more important, though, are the truths about God's nature as revealed in the teachings of the Bible and incarnated in the life of Jesus Christ.

Much about God remains a mystery. Were God fully explainable, divinity would cease to exist. Nevertheless, God wills that people understand something of the divine nature. That divine desire motivates revelation. You can know more than enough about God to find comfort, strength, and hope while trying to cope with all kinds of difficulties.

No one can say all that needs to be said about God. Everyone, however, can confess a few certainties. You can claim each of these theological truths as a personal reality.

"God is love. God loves me." More than simply one of God's admirable attributes, love constitutes the essential nature of God. No situation stands outside God's compassion. No individual exists as an exemption from God's love for all people.

You do not have to beg God to love you. God loves all of us personally and unconditionally. We cannot do anything—not one thing—that causes God to stop loving us. As Paul triumphantly concluded, nothing, not anything "in all creation, will be able to separate us from the love of God in Christ Jesus our Lord" (Rom. 8:39).

"God is good. God desires my good." God wills good for all people. Again, no exceptions. A love-based desire for good among all persons forms an integral part of the divine nature.

Crises can cause us to lose sight of this fundamental truth. Trouble-plagued people commonly ask, "Why is God doing this to me?" The question is as unfortunate as it is predictable. Such an inquiry implies a less-than-Christian view of God.

No one can satisfactorily explain why bad things happen. However, everyone can be certain that God neither wills nor causes tragic circumstances in people's lives. God wills good. God wills health, not sickness; joy, not hurt; fellowship, not alienation; life, not death.

You can see the strength of God's will for good dramatized in God's willingness to enter bad situations and God's ability to work with even the worst experiences of life to create the possibility of some benefit coming from them. That does not mean God causes critical problems to exist in order to have a backdrop against which to do good works. Not at all. What happened in the crucifixion of Jesus exemplifies what happens again and again in our own lives. God becomes a part of a horrendous situation, even one fraught with despicable evil, and lovingly remains within it until a possibility exists that some good can come out of it.

The good that God wills for the world, God also wills for you.

"God is mercy. God is merciful to me." God makes you the beneficiary of divine mercy. You do not have to ask for it. You do not even have to recognize your need for it. God's mercy is a gift.

God doesn't play games with mercy—refusing to offer mercy unless people privately request it, assume a prescribed posture and display a proper attitude, or publicly declare their need for it in the words of a tradition-shaped creed. God refuses to make mercy contingent on any human language or behavior, merits or promises. God acts mercifully because mercy constitutes God's nature.

Poetic words from Frederick W. Faber beautifully capture this basic truth about God. In a hymn entitled "There's a Wideness in God's Mercy," Faber warns that we make God's love "too narrow/By false limits of our own" and magnify God's strictness with a zeal God "will not own." Then the poet offers a fundamental assertion of unchangeable certainty: "For the love of God is broader/Than the measure of one's mind;/And the heart of the Eternal/Is most wonderfully kind."[1]

"What happens then?" you ask. "If this loving God wills my good and offers me mercy, why can't I just trust in God to get me through this difficulty and know God will do it?" Not a bad question.

Jesus reveals God's respect for human freedom—a divine desire that every individual function as a free person rather than as a mechanical marionette controlled by a heavenly puppeteer. All people make decisions within the context of God-given freedom. Yet not all people care about your plight. Thus, pragmatically, you cannot expect everyone to act in your best interests. Theologically, you cannot assume God will manipulate persons to work for your good.

"So what can I expect from God while I try to cope with this crisis?" you want to know. Another good question with a tremendously important answer.

You can count on God's enabling you to function at your best in the face of difficulties. Jesus demonstrated that God will provide comfort for your hurt, reassurance for your disappointments, forgiveness for your sins, direction upon request, and strength to sustain your efforts at coping.

God loves you, wills your good, and relates to you in mercy. But at no time, not even in a crisis, can you sit back and expect God to do everything for you. To believe otherwise involves bad theology and leaves you without any strategy for coping with difficulties.

Deal with Your Guilt

Guilt and crises go hand in hand, sometimes justifiably. Acts of sinfulness that precipitate a crisis also create guilt. In other instances, though, the two unite without reason. A crisis erupts apart from any evidence of immorality—a business fails or a parent dies. An explanation for what happens may exist (poor management in the case of the business or a parent's bad health), but, if so, it is completely unrelated to any evil intent or action. When people experience guilt in such a situation, as they often do (asking, "What wrong have I have done to bring about this misfortune?"), the problem is superficial guilt, not real guilt. Neither kind of guilt—superficial or real—though, can legitimately occupy a place in a life of faith.

Superficial guilt diminishes, if it does not dissolve completely, when examined under the bright light of truth. If a sense of guilt adds to the load you carry in a crisis, appraise your feelings honestly. Are you plagued by a nagging residue from an ill-informed family tradition, stabs of pain formed by social mores that have been violated, or regrets related to personal failures that have become confused with acts that betray your moral consciousness? None of that qualifies as guilt. Be done with feeling guilty for such reasons.

Real guilt stems from an awareness of wrongdoing. You do not have to endure even real guilt, however. In fact, you should not. Guilt lasts only as long as you ignore or reject divine forgiveness. Authentic faith readily accepts God's unmerited grace and joyfully frolics in the freedom that follows grace's removal of guilt.

Typically, reactions to guilt fall into one of two categories. Some folks become obsessed with guilt, assuming that a sense of guilt represents a sensitive spirituality. Other individuals ignore guilt entirely, refusing to give it any credibility. Both of these extreme reactions represent serious spiritual errors.

Real guilt deserves attention. Guilt produced by wrongdoing serves as a warning, a means of instruction, an indication that life has taken a course that needs correction. But no person should allow guilt to become an obsession. Long-term unrelieved guilt stems not from the gospel but from imposters of the gospel. The good news Jesus heralded in words and deeds relentlessly applies a scalpel to guilt and compassionately removes it from a person's soul.

Exercising faith requires dealing with guilt. Whether superficial or real, sustained guilt does not belong in your life. Learn from your guilt, then be done with it. Coping abilities can be strengthened and spiritual health fully enjoyed only after guilt has been eradicated.

Accept Forgiveness

You will fail to experience forgiveness only if you refuse to accept forgiveness, either from God or from yourself.

Strangely, forgiving ourselves often constitutes more of a problem than receiving forgiveness from God. No question exists about divine forgiveness. God readily pardons people who honestly acknowledge their sins within the relationship of divine-human love. We accept the reality of that forgiveness because we trust God completely.

Forgiving ourselves is another matter. Misunderstanding and confusion add to the difficulty of self-forgiveness. A man mourns, "If I had exercised greater faith, I would not have committed this wrong." He refuses to forgive himself for wrongdoing, concluding that he does not deserve pardon and imagining that denying himself forgiveness represents a noble sacrifice for his sin. Similarly, a woman is mired in the quicksand of a smothering guilt, bearing a shame she can satisfy only by self-punishment.

Remember, literally everyone needs forgiveness at one time or another. Everyone sins.

"But my sin was worse than most," you protest sadly. Not so. Sin is sin. Sins cannot be ranked in order of severity. Sin is disobedience to God. Every act of disobedience to God is serious.

Your sins and failures reveal the nature of your humanity more than they show a weakness in your faith. God understands your sins. And God forgives your sins, all of them. Claim God's forgiveness. And while you are at it, act on the assurance that if God can forgive you, every reason exists for you to forgive yourself. Do it.

Affirm Struggle

The presence of a crisis does not indicate a failure of faith. Struggle pervades the life of faith.

Outstanding personalities identified in the Bible as people of faith lived as pilgrims who experienced struggles throughout their spiritual journeys. Abraham struggled with honesty. Habakkuk encountered doubt. Naomi and Ruth worked hard to resolve issues of loyalty. Jeremiah fought depression. In the New Testament, Paul battled a physical problem, Peter wrestled with fiery emotions, and Timothy struggled with tradition.

Do not fear spiritual struggle. Consider it indicative of a failure of faith, or feel you must apologize for it. Faith embraces struggle.

Even the most devoted of God's people live with struggles—moral struggles as well as theological and relational skirmishes. Most of us identify completely with the confession: "For I do not do the good I want, but the evil I do not want is what I do" (Rom 7:19). The painfully familiar words come from Paul, the apostle from Tarsus, who identified himself as the chief of sinners. An absence of moral struggle usually signals spiritual death.

Doubts provide no reason for despair. As long as they are transitional rather than permanent, doubts can serve as avenues to greater faith. No need exists for you to deny or seek to repress doubts, fearing them as affronts to faith. Honest faith affirms questions and appreciates challenges. Raise your questions about faith. Examine all your thoughts that challenge faith. Truth never destroys real faith.

Nurture Your Faith

Spiritual health, like physical health, requires nurture. Faith needs encouragement, insight, inspiration, and instruction. Your spirit longs to be fed.

Traditional spiritual disciplines continue to have great value. You can find spiritual sustenance in reading the Bible. Virtually every crisis you will ever encounter has a precedent among people discussed in the Bible. King David ran the gamut of emotions before being crushed by the dissolution of his family. Paul struggled with limitations and battled frustrations caused by a physical difficulty. Jeremiah, the ancient prophet, faced a grinding depression. Disciples of Jesus experienced a near-crippling grief. Habakkuk complained of doubts. Mary, the mother of Jesus, pondered many perplexing questions of faith. Studying the scriptures can yield profoundly helpful insights into how you can best deal with a wide range of problems.

Regularly participating in corporate worship provides you with human fellowship and keeps you in touch with the transcendent God who lovingly joins you in all situations. According to historic catechisms repeated by church people through the ages, you are never truer to your most basic nature than when lost in the work of worship. Though authentic worship is an end in itself (if not, real worship does not occur), acts of worship invariably result in benefits for worshipers. For example, when you worship God, you learn how to reconcile the vertical and horizontal dimensions of life, discover resources of strength that are never found apart from worship, and experience a communion (human and divine) that assures you of never having to face a crisis alone. Confidence grows strong in a context of true worship as you realize that God meets all your pleas for help and requests for forgiveness with a rush of grace. Peace ensues.

Offering your talents as a means for ministry to others reminds you of your worth as an instrument of care. You begin to understand the meaning of those biblical words that previously had sounded like double-talk—how a person receives by giving, wins by losing, and lives by dying. Faith thrives and grows strong in service.

You may find benefit as well in times of silent meditation. Sitting quietly and pondering how your faith in God relates to your hurting body, depressed spirit, or troubled conscience can prove extremely helpful. Sometimes aids to spiritual development can enhance your enjoyment of solitude—reflecting on religious art, examining the texts of great hymns of faith, and studying the meaning of Christian symbols. Feed your faith regularly just as you do your body.

Coping with crises usually necessitates making cutbacks in our normal activities. Some routine concerns have to be set aside until the time of trouble has passed. Activities that nurture faith do not qualify as expendable items, however, even for the briefest of periods. Crises drain us spiritually as well as physically. Tough conditions force actions that expend great amounts of energy, set emotions on edge, and consume huge blocks of time. Amid crises, faith-nurturing actions take on more importance than ever.

Live in Grace

Recently a pastor invited me to lunch to ask me the question, "Do you believe in restoration?" When I requested a bit of elaboration on the meaning of his inquiry, this religious leader told me of a man (a former pastor who is a friend of his) who committed a sin that resulted in great personal turmoil, financial loss, and social criticism. My host wanted to know if I thought it would be worthwhile to offer help to his friend and maybe even try to reclaim him as a minister in the church.

My response to him was affirmation and encouragement. "Sure, I believe in restoration. Nothing could be more compatible with the nature of the gospel or essential in the lives of people who believe the gospel. I hope you will proceed with helping this fellow." Internally, though, I screamed, Why do you have to ask that question? You—a minister of the gospel—of all people! If Christianity is not about working for the restoration of troubled people, what is it about?

My lunchtime host gave voice to a much too prevalent problem. Many folks affirm grace as a doctrinal truth that makes salvation possible while failing to incorporate grace into their daily activities as the primary principle governing both the personal and communal life of people of faith. Please avoid that problem. Grace exists for the whole of the spiritual journey, not just for its start. Live in grace—and by grace.

Redemption is a reality. Grace abounds. Claim that grace for yourself and extend that grace to others. As you do, be aware that not all people (not even all "church people") will respond in kind. Some folks hoard grace mercilessly. Others discount grace as an absolute impracticality. Those people do not represent the thrust of Christianity. Refuse to allow graceless people to determine how you will live.

"All this talk about grace and faith sounds too good to be true," you say. Your comment may be influenced by the misguided though popular thought that fears grace is a source of license and thus declares judgment-saturated bad news to be more religious than good news. Regardless of its source, however, your remark is in order. You are right.

For most of us Jesus is a sight for sore eyes, the sound of the gospel is difficult for our ears to hear, and grace seems like wishful thinking. But, that is precisely the nature of the gospel, which inspires and gives content to the Christian faith. From beginning to end, the gospel is good news, news so good we have a hard time believing it can be true.

God offers you good news even in bad times. The only thing worse than not believing this good news—the good news of the gospel—is believing it and not living by it.

Exercise faith.

CHAPTER TEN

Offer Help to Someone Else

As you progress in coping with a crisis, a time will come when you need to consider how—and whether—you can be helpful to other troubled people. No one can determine that time for you. You can be sure such a moment has not arrived, however, if you still need critical help for yourself. At that point, your most responsible actions continue to be taking care of yourself and coping with your own difficulties.

After a while, though, refusing to serve as a helpful resource to other people rivals expending the totality of your energy on other people as unwise, uncaring, and debilitating. If we never look beyond ourselves during our journeys toward health and wholeness, in all probability we will either get into more trouble, become ill again, or stop short of the goal marked by recovery and stability.

Generally, pained people become hypersensitive to other pained people. Not always, though. Sometimes pain drives an individual into a shell. Prolonged pain prompts an embittered, self-centered retreat from life accompanied only by complete disinterest in others. But insensitivity to pain constitutes the exception rather than the rule among individuals who have endured suffering.

Most likely, your pain will make you unusually aware of pain in other persons. Having been there yourself, the demeanor and facial expressions of a friend cause you to know instinctively, "He is really hurting." That kind of quickened sensitivity empowers in you a unique ability to help people besieged by crises.

Caution!

As you emerge from a crisis in your own life, exercise caution before entering someone else's crisis. This encouragement of caution has nothing to do with an uncaring attitude, "keeping your distance," or shying away from involvement with a troubled person. Rather, caution before actions aimed at helping someone else allows you to engage in self-examination dedicated to the other person's welfare as well as to your own. You have no business seeking to help anybody else as long as you desperately need help for yourself. Even beyond that situation, however, a careful determination of your motivations and credentials for helping should precede any efforts to be of assistance to others.

Examine your motivations for offering help. Be careful here. This can be tricky. How on earth can efforts to help a troubled person be anything but good? you ask. Please don't doubt it. Ill-inspired actions camouflaged as "help" can result in much more harm than good.

Long before they are far enough along in coping with their own problems or recovering sufficient health to be of assistance to anyone else, some persons begin to offer help to other people. All too often these efforts aim at establishing self-worth, experiencing self-gratification, and gaining affirmation for themselves or escaping their own difficulties. Actions disguised as offers of helpfulness actually represent symptoms of extreme selfishness.

Occasionally a troubled person tests certain coping procedures by commending them to others and then observing the results. What works for a friend is then applied personally. What fails to help a friend is disregarded. Watch out! In this sick scenario, counsel that may even have a ring of compassion and competence about it actually transforms people into "lab rats" for the benefit of the troubled imposter "helper."

Danger abounds in all help-related efforts spawned by a troubled person. In addition to conveying harmful misinformation, the "helper" can set up unhealthy dependency patterns. In the process, the recipient of "help"—a vulnerable person at best—may find his or her emotions manipulated and body prostituted. A hurting person is used for the benefit of an individual claiming to be a "helper" who is, in reality, another (maybe desperately) hurting person. Caution!

Check your credentials for offering help. Keep your limitations clearly in focus. Hurt can sensitize you to troubled people and enable you to identify with their plight. Empathy, however, cannot suffice as a substitute for professional expertise. Previous experience in coping with a crisis does not qualify you to act as a diagnostician, to prescribe medication, to function as a therapist, or even to outline the best course of action for any other person. To ignore the limits of your ability to help others sets up the possibility of your "help" contributing to tragedy.

Reach Out with Compassion

A humorous image makes a serious point. Remember the Boy Scout who insisted on taking an elderly woman to the other side of the street when she didn't want to cross. That is not help.

Genuine help means reaching out to a troubled person with an offer of unconditional compassion. Regardless of how much you feel able to give in the way of insights, directions, and recommendations, refrain from forcing yourself on people, showering them with unrequested counsel, and pressuring them to take actions they oppose. Reach out to troubled folks with no more (but no less) than compassion. Such an approach to those who hurt respects the personhood of each individual and provides all people the freedom to request help or remain silent without fear of rebuke.

Many times when plagued by near-unbearable hurts, a person wants nothing more than the relational support of a caring friend. No advice. No strong arm. No entertainment. Not even an attempt at identification by means of saying, "I understand." Just presence, the quiet presence of a friend whose care is beyond question and devoid of conditions.

Real help necessitates accepting people where they are and responding to the needs they define. Approaching hurting persons with efforts to fit them into your categories of need and assistance—"I know you think this is what you want, but let me tell you what you really need"—is never beneficial. Help requires flexibility and adaptability. Compassion mandates a minimum interest in the program of assistance you feel you can offer to anyone and maximum responsiveness to a specific troubled person's pleas for help.

Listen with Understanding

Hurting people need to be heard. They do not, however, need a listener who tells them how to speak and instructs them on what they should and should not say.

When listening to a troubled person, refrain from interrupting with corrections and instructions. Avoid making comments such as "You really need to collect your thoughts and speak more coherently," "This problem does not justify your high level of emotion," "I wish you would lower your voice," or "Don't mumble." Once an individual begins to articulate the hurt, don't stop or try to control this flow of speech. That does more harm than good. Besides, as a distraught man pointed out to me a long time ago, "A person who is not hurting has no right to tell a person who *is* hurting how loud to holler."

If you want to help a troubled person, listen intently. Listen to that person's screams, whispers, curses, prayers. And listen to silence.

Once you have been through a crisis and had some degree of success in coping with it, you face a persistent temptation to make everyone in trouble a beneficiary of the insights and wisdom gained from your experience. Listening becomes difficult because you have so much you want to pass along that you are certain others need to hear. Repeatedly you want to say, I said the same thing or I felt that way also, and then declare, Let me tell you how to handle that. Halt! To be helpful to those who hurt, you must exercise discipline and restraint. You must give the person in trouble the right to set the agenda for conversation.

If you do all the talking when visiting with a person in need, you will probably end up feeling very good about the abundance of helpful counsel you have offered. But the individual in need will feel no better, will perhaps develop resentment over your know-it-all demeanor, and for sure will sense an even stronger desire to be heard, to encounter someone more interested in listening than in talking.

Do Not Pass Judgments

Passing moral judgments about a person's actions fails to qualify as help. When preachments replace empathetic listening, most likely your presence with a person in trouble is no longer needed.

I have a friend with a Moses complex. He feels compelled to serve as an oracle of the law, giving the impression at any moment that he has just descended from Mount Sinai. In his mind, no uncertainty exists about the exact law in need of elaboration in every situation. Thus, when this fellow seeks to help hurting people, he seldom succeeds.

Though my friend sincerely wants to assist folks in trouble, he views listening as a waste of time. Typically, after hearing two or three comments describing a person's difficulty, my friend dogmatically asserts, "You have a sin problem, that's all." Then comes his lecture: "If you will just heed the teachings of the Bible and get your life right with God, everything will be all right." He has his say. The hurting person stops speaking, puts up strong defenses, and feigns listening to prevent more pain. No help occurs.

You cannot know the moral dynamics at work in another

person's life. You may think you do, but you don't. Judging intentions and motivations, distinguishing between a lack of wisdom and a bent toward evil, and determining guilt and innocence require a competence that greatly exceeds any individual's abilities. No wonder Christian scriptures convey the recurrent mandate not to judge other people ("Do not judge"—Matt. 7:1; Luke 6:37; see also Rom. 2:1).

Before offering a discourse on morality to a person struggling with a crisis, clarify the motivation behind your moral declaration. Are you trying to serve the person in trouble or satisfy a need of your own? Neither moral positioning on your part nor voicing moral judgments aimed at the sufferer makes a helpful contribution to alleviating hurt.

Offer Encouragement, Support, and Hope

At times you will be able to help a crisis-plagued friend in very specific ways—picking up a mother's children at school one afternoon so she can see a doctor, fulfilling an obligation at a charitable agency when the volunteer does not feel like leaving his house. If the relationship between the two of you is a good one, your friend will tell you in detail the kind of help that is needed. Apart from this, though, you can still function as an invaluable helper for a friend in trouble—offering tokens of continuing support, providing symbols of hope, and speaking words of encouragement.

Daily needs vary dramatically as a person tries to hold on during the wild emotional roller-coaster ride so integral to coping with a major crisis. A real helper seeks to understand and respond to the specific relational needs of a troubled person on any given day.

In an attempt to encourage a discouraged friend, however, do not promise more than you can deliver. Ultimately, overstating your ability to help will only worsen the person's plight. Likewise, in the interest of nurturing hope, refrain from holding out false hopes. Generating hopes that you know cannot possibly be fulfilled only creates unrealistic expectations that eventually lead to greater despair.

In a sensitive way, say all that can legitimately be said to help a person in trouble. But no more. And when nothing can be said, be sure your presence communicates a strength of enduring support for the person that helps in ways words can never equal.

Facilitate More Help

Often you can best help a person in trouble by getting that person in contact with a professional caregiver. Most people are reticent about admitting needs, much less requesting help, regardless of the difficulties they face. When you provide specific information about a professional who can help a hurting friend and affirm the wisdom of making contact with that person, you provide a service of inestimable value.

At this point, words forged in your own personal experience may prove beneficial. You can provide a great service by saying to a disturbed individual trying to decide whether or not to ask for help, "Amid my struggles, I finally realized I had to have help beyond what I was getting from my family and friends. This doctor was a godsend for me. I'm quite sure she can help you as well. Here are her name, address, and phone number. If you want me to help you get in touch with her, just let me know."

Often a hurting friend will not immediately accept your advice and act on your suggestions. Please do not abandon your friend if that happens. Stand by quietly and lovingly. A referral for help rejected the first time it is offered may well be accepted later. Be there to repeat the information when and if your pained friend requests it.

Perfection is not a prerequisite for helpfulness. Thank God. Were that the case, the world would be without helpers. Your mistakes, sins, and wounds allow you to benefit a troubled person in ways unattainable for people who imagine themselves above it all. Generally, the best help for folks who hurt comes either from other persons who have known great hurt or from professionals academically trained in the dynamics of pain.

You will not always know exactly what to do or precisely what to say when relating to people with problems. Do not fret about that. More importantly, don't allow feelings of inadequacy to keep you from individuals in need. Chances are that your very presence as a compassionate, nonthreatening friend will be more than enough to provide comfort and reassurance.

As you resolve to help others, commit yourself to a variation of the golden rule. Determine that you will help troubled people as you would want to be helped yourself. In relating to individuals in need, focus on the actions by which other people have most helped you during your times of trouble or on what you most wish someone had done to help you. Pay attention to your own hurt. Your personal pilgrimage of pain can provide powerful instruction in how you can best help others who hurt.

Helping other people does not mark the end of your dealing with problems in your own life. You can, and should, continue to receive help for your own hurts even as you attempt to ease the pain in other people. If times come when old difficulties resurface or new problems arise to dominate your thoughts and feelings, put helping others on hold for a period. Take care of yourself. Bracketing times to deal with your own needs will only serve to increase the opportunities you have to help others and the abilities with which you can claim those opportunities.

Focusing on what can be gained for yourself by giving help to someone else creates the poorest possible reason for offering assistance to others. Stay away from such an approach to service. Genuine help cares only about improvement in the one who hurts.

OFFER HELP TO SOMEONE ELSE

In reality, though, people who practice selfless helpfulness discover, usually serendipitously, that they too benefit from what they give. Keep the proper order in mind. If you help others while looking for a reward, you will probably not find it. Help others for the sole purpose of being helpful, and you may be surprised by joy.

Offer help to someone else.

EPILOGUE

Few people find quick solutions to their problems. You are not likely to be an exception. Coping resembles running a long-distance race.

Most crises with traceable causes develop from harmful thoughts, abused feelings, and ill-advised actions that have existed for many years. Such thoughts, feelings, and actions accumulated over a long period of time and took their collective shape slowly. In all probability, they will not disappear rapidly. Nor will the crises they have produced go away overnight.

At some point, professional help may be needed to achieve the adjustments, health, and wholeness you desire as the end results of coping with a crisis. Please do not hesitate to seek such help. Reaching out to highly trained helpers who can aid your efforts at coping in no way demonstrates inferior spirituality. Skilled doctors who can guide us through physical, mental, and emotional crises function as gifts from God. You display promising wisdom as well as abiding faith by drawing upon their expertise.

Recovering from the trauma induced by a crisis does not usually involve a straight line of success. A back-and-forth, up-and-down, zigzag pattern of development is most common. One day you will make good progress. On another day you will regress. Do not become discouraged. Such fluctuations are normal. Keep moving. With God's help and assistance from other people, persist in your efforts to cope.

Many times over the past several years, in crisis moments, I have returned to words written by a popular preacher of another day. Every time I read them, these comments strike me as

EPILOGUE

helpful words from God. They give me sustenance for continuing what seems to be the endless work of coping. Perhaps they can benefit you as well and serve as a source of the strength that makes endurance possible.

On his first time back in the pulpit after his wife's tragic death, the notable preacher Arthur John Gossip delivered a sermon entitled "But When Life Tumbles In, What Then?" Gossip's sermon reflected the personal struggle he experienced in relating faith specifically to the untimely loss of his spouse. But the general substance of this minister's remarks applies to any one of a thousand different crises—crises that we experience.

Against a backdrop comprised of insights into the travail of a soul, using words from the character named Hopeful in John Bunyan's *The Pilgrim's Progress,* Gossip concluded his message with a confession of faith. The comments from this hurting herald of good news lift up my heart even when coping with a prolonged crisis has burdened me with weariness and discouragement. I end this book with Gossip's conclusion because, most days, it is also mine.

"I don't think you need be afraid of life. Our hearts are very frail; and there are places where the road is very steep and very lonely. But we have a wonderful God. And as Paul puts it, what can separate us from His love? Not death, he says immediately, pushing that aside at once as the most obvious of all impossibilities.

No, not death. For, standing in the roaring of the Jordan, cold to the heart with its dreadful chill, and very conscious of the terror of its rushing, I too, like Hopeful, can call back to you who one day in your turn will have to cross it, 'Be of good cheer . . . for I feel the bottom, and it is sound.' "[1]

NOTES

Chapter 1: Be Honest About Your Situation

1. Each of these approaches to a problem is discussed in Stephen Grunlan and Daniel Lambrides, *Healing Relationships: A Christian's Manual for Lay Counseling* (Camp Hill, Pa.: Christian Publications, 1984), pp. 63–65.

2. In his widely respected research, William Glasser found that the one common factor among persons experiencing mental illness was an avoidance of truth. Yet the truth they feared would destroy them was actually a potential source of healing. Numerous other professionals, including Freud, have made similar findings. David G. Benner, *Healing Emotional Wounds* (Grand Rapids: Baker Book House, 1990), p. 89.

3. Cited in Norman Cousins, *Anatomy of an Illness as Perceived by the Patient: Reflections on Healing and Regeneration* (New York: Bantam Books, 1981), pp. 65–66.

4. Harold Kushner, *When All You've Ever Wanted Isn't Enough: The Search for a Life That Matters* (New York: Summit Books, 1986), p. 91.

Chapter 2: Get Plenty of Rest

1. Mary Ella Stuart, *To Bend Without Breaking: Stress and How to Deal with It* (Nashville: Abingdon Press, 1977), p. 94.

Chapter 3: Reach Out to Friends

1. Donald E. Demaray, *Laughter, Joy, and Healing* (Grand Rapids: Baker Book House, 1986), p. 221, citing a research report printed in the *American Journal of Epidemiology*.

2. Mary Ella Stuart, *To Bend Without Breaking: Stress and How to Deal with It* (Nashville: Abingdon Press, 1977), p. 96.

3. This idea comes from Martin Marty, *Friendship* (Allen, Tex.: Argus Communications, 1980), p. 129. In this excellent treatise on friendship, Marty asserts (p. 108), "Anyone who has ever known a friend or been a friend may find almost nothing in life more significant."

Chapter 4: Fight Cynicism

1. Norman Cousins described this incident in an untitled, unpublished address on the occasion of his reception of the Albert Schweitzer Award from Johns Hopkins University, Baltimore, Maryland, October 18, 1990.

2. This statement, by Dr. Irving Oyle, is cited in Donald E. Demaray, *Laughter, Joy, and Healing* (Grand Rapids: Baker Book House, 1986), p. 56.

Chapter 5: Keep A Sense of Humor

1. Work, dependence on friends, and prayer constitute the other three coping devices that Sheehy discusses. The other four stress-related coping mechanisms that receive attention in Vaillant's work are anticipation, altruism, repression, and sublimation. Allen Klein, *The Healing Power of Humor: Techniques for Getting Through Loss, Setbacks, Upsets, Disappointments, Difficulties, Trials, Tribulations, and All That Not-So-Funny Stuff* (Los Angeles: Jeremy P. Tarcher, 1989), p. 7.

2. Vera M. Robinson records this comment in the second volume of *Handbook of Humor Research,* cited in Donald E. Demaray, *Laughter, Joy, and Healing* (Grand Rapids: Baker Book House, 1986), p. 105.

3. Demaray, *Laughter, Joy, and Healing,* p. 13.

4. Robert E. Neale in "The Crucifixion as Play," a chapter appended to Jurgen Moltmann's *Theology of Play,* trans. Reinhard Ulrich (New York: Harper & Row, 1972), p. 84.

5. Norman Cousins, *Anatomy of an Illness as Perceived by the Patient: Reflections on Healing and Regeneration* (New York: Bantam Books, 1981). Commenting on the power of laughter in his experience, Cousins wrote (p. 39), "I made the joyous discovery that ten minutes of genuine belly laughter had an anesthetic effect and would give me at least two hours of pain-free sleep."

6. Victor E. Frankl, *Man's Search for Meaning: An Introduction to Logotherapy,* trans. Ilse Lasch (New York: Washington Square Press, 1963), pp. 69–71.

7. Demaray, *Laughter, Joy, and Healing,* p. 13.

8. Klein, *The Healing Power of Humor,* p. 166.

9. Emmett Kelly with F. Beverly Kelley, *Clown* (New York: Prentice-Hall, 1954), p. 126. See also C. Welton Gaddy, *God's Clowns: Messengers of the Good News* (San Francisco: Harper & Row, 1990), pp. 65–71.

Chapter 6: Pray

1. Quoted in George A. Buttrick, *The Power of Prayer Today* (Waco, Tex.: Word Books, 1975), p. 17.

2. William S. Sadler, *The Practice of Psychiatry* (St. Louis: G. V. Mosby Co., 1953), cited in Walter G. Muelder, "The Efficacy of Prayer," in *Healing, Human and Divine: Man's Search for Health and Wholeness Through Science, Faith, and Prayer,* ed. Simon Doniger (New York: Association Press, 1957), p. 131.

3. Buttrick, *The Power of Prayer Today,* p. 51.

4. Howard Thurman, *With Head and Heart: The Autobiog-*

raphy of Howard Thurman (New York: Harcourt Brace Jovanovich, 1979), p. 122.

5. Quoted in Don E. Saliers, *Worship and Spirituality* (Philadelphia: Westminster Press, 1984), p. 28.

6. Robert Moats Miller, *Harry Emerson Fosdick: Preacher, Pastor, Prophet* (New York: Oxford University Press, 1985), p. 71.

7. The floating analogy is taken from John H. Westerhoff III, *A Pilgrim People: Learning Through the Church Year* (Minneapolis: Seabury Press, 1984), p. 49.

Chapter 7: Channel Your Anger

1. Barry Bailey, *Living With Your Feelings* (Nashville: Abingdon Press, 1980), p. 28.

2. Lewis B. Smedes, *Forgive and Forget: Healing the Hurts We Don't Deserve* (San Francisco: Harper & Row, 1984), p. 108.

3. With Curtis Mitchell, Iris Bolton narrates this story of tragedy and triumph in *My Son . . . My Son . . .: A Guide to Healing After Death, Loss, or Suicide,* 12th ed. (Atlanta: Bolton Press, 1991).

Chapter 8: Renew Your Dreams

1. Milenko Matanovic, *Meandering Rivers and Square Tomatoes: The Art of Crafting Visions* (Israquah, Wash.: Morningtown Press, 1988), pp. 1–2.

Chapter 9: Exercise Faith

1. Frederick William Faber, "There's a Wideness in God's Mercy," *The Baptist Hymnal,* ed. Wesley L. Forbis (Nashville: Convention Press, 1991), p. 25.

Epilogue

1. Arthur John Gossip, "When Life Tumbles In, What Then?" in *Twenty Centuries of Great Preaching*, ed. Clyde E. Fant, Jr., and William M. Pinson, Jr., vol. 8, pp. 238–239.